Native Woody Landscape and Restoration Plants of the Eastern United States

Michael L. Dorn

Shore Publications

Native Woody Landscape and Restoration Plants of the Eastern United States
By Michael L. Dorn
Copyright Michael L. Dorn© 2010

First Edition Pulished by Shore Publications, 145 River Street, Adah, PA 15410.
Produced in the United States of America

ISBN: 978-0-938833-39-0

All rights reserved. No part of this publication may be reproduced, stored in a computer, or transmitted in any form without the written consent of the author.

All Shore Publications titles at: www.ohiopyle.info
Contact: shorepublications@yahoo.com

Contact Michael Dorn for speaking presentations at: 864-324-4040 or mchdrn@aol.com

Order Online: www.nativeplantbook.com or www.ohiopyle.info

ACKNOWLEDGEMENTS

    I would like to thank my parents for their love and support over the years; they have helped make all of my accomplishments possible. I would like to thank all of my professors and lab instructors from Clemson University for the wonderful education that I was given. I would like to thank the nurseries and landscape businesses that have help me prosper. My sincere appreciation goes to all of my clients for their business the last several years.

    I'd like to give a special thanks to the following: Frank Brezeale, Bill Head and Head Lee Nursery, Dr. David Bradshaw, Dr. Ted Whitwell, Mary Haque, and Susanne Byrd. Finally, I'd like to thank Marci McGuinness and Shore Publications for believing in this book and making it available for all to enjoy.

CONTENTS

Preface v

Introduction vi

Trees 1

Shrubs 36

Vines 82

Native Woody Plants for Wet Sites, Stream-banks, and Shorelines 89

Native Woody Plants for Dry Sites 90

Native Woody Plants with Showy Flowers 91

Native Woody Plants with Showy Fruits 93

Native Woody Plants with Attractive Fall Color 94

Native Woody Plants that are Evergreen 95

Native Woody Plants that Provide Wildlife Food 96

USDA Hardiness Zones Map 97

Glossary 98

Bibliography 100

Index to Botanical Names 101

Index to Common Names 103

About the Author 106

PREFACE

My passion for the natural ecology of the Southeastern United States, as well as my experience using native plants, has inspired me to write a book about native woody plant materials. Native plants can play an important role in the landscape, especially when trying to blend traditional landscapes with surrounding natural areas. They offer great possibility and provide magnificent beauty in the form of flowers, fruits, and fall leaf color. In addition, most projects involving mitigation, stabilization, or buffering require the use of native plants for permit approval. The planting of native species is becoming and will continue to become more prevalent in today's landscapes and ecosystems.

It is important to have literature that will showcase the aesthetics and functionality of native plants. I intend for this book to serve as both encouragement for the use of native species as well as a valuable reference to homeowners, students, and the plant industry.

INTRODUCTION

The use of native plants in the landscape has become more common in recent years. With the increasing demand for lower maintenance and less water use, native plants will continue to play an important role in the landscape and nursery industry. In addition, native plants are one of the key ingredients in restoration, naturalizing, mitigation, and/or erosion control practices. The use of native plants has the potential to provide several benefits. Plants native to a given region are adapted to the conditions of that region; therefore they tend to require less maintenance than exotic species. Natives also pose less potential for becoming a nuisance species, and they have the ability to enhance or restore landscapes, natural areas, shorelines, stream-banks, wetlands, woodlands, and other ecosystems. The purpose of this book is to provide homeowners, designers, contractors, students, and nurseries with color photos and useful information that describes many of the native plants of the Eastern United States.

The plants featured in this book are grouped into one of three categories: Trees, Shrubs, or Vines. This book does not include every native woody plant that exists in the Eastern United States, but rather the ones that I feel provide the most aesthetic and functional value for the landscape setting as well as for stabilization, restoration, and/or mitigation practices. This book will make it easy for readers to find out how and where to use the plant materials by identifying the physical characteristics, the culture, the aesthetics, and the ecological value of the plants.

TREES

Acer rubrum - Red Maple

Red Maple is one of my favorite trees. If given ample moisture, these trees thrive and offer intense fall leaf color in a wide variety of orange and red hues. This is a great tree for framing a landscape by planting one on each front corner of a property. Red Maple can also be used as a specimen or a shade tree, and it is ideal for shorelines.

PLANT TYPE: Deciduous, broadleaf, large tree
MATURE SIZE: 40-60' in height and 20-40' in width
LEAVES: Opposite, simple, 3-5 lobed; green leaves in summer turn orange, red, and purple in the fall
BARK: Smooth, gray turning dark gray and rough at maturity
FLOWERS: Red, bloom in late winter-early spring before leaves emerge
FRUIT: Reddish, winged samara, turns brown at maturity
HARDINESS: Zones 4-8; due to the large range in hardiness, it is best to select a local ecotype
FORM/SHAPE: Pyramidal in youth, oval to rounded at maturity
GROWTH RATE: Moderate to fast
SOIL: Tolerates a range of soils, but performs best in a moist, slightly acidic, humus rich soil; tolerates wet sites
LIGHT REQUIREMENTS: Full sun to part shade; best growth and color in full sun
DISEASE PROBLEMS: Anthracnose, canker rot, leaf blight, nematodes, powdery mildew, and *Verticillium* wilt
INSECT PROBLEMS: Mapleworm, caterpillars, bagworm, leaf miner, mites, mealybugs, scale, aphids, and thrips
LANDSCAPE VALUE: Shade tree, specimen tree, buffers, mitigation, shoreline/stream-bank restoration, and naturalizing; excellent fall color
PRUNING TIME: Late winter – early spring
CULTIVARS: There are more than 50 cultivars; the following are some of the most common. Autumn Flame® - early red fall color; October Glory® - late orange to red fall color; Red Sunset® - orange to red fall color; Summer Red® – new growth is burgundy to red in summer, fall color yellow; tolerant of high heat; 'V. J. Drake' – fall color starts with a red leaf margin with green in the middle

Acer saccharum - Sugar Maple

The picture best showcases what this tree has to offer. This large shade tree brightens the fall sky with various yellow and orange colored leaves. Although it is found in the south, it prefers cooler regions. Sugar Maple is a good food source for wildlife.

PLANT TYPE: Deciduous, broadleaf, large tree
MATURE SIZE: 40-80' in height and 20-40' in width
LEAVES: Opposite, simple, 3-5 lobed; dark green leaves in summer turn yellow, orange, and sometimes red in the fall
BARK: Smooth, gray-brown turning blackish gray with deep furrows at maturity
FLOWERS: Light green, bloom in spring before leaves emerge
FRUIT: Light green, winged samara, turns brown at maturity
HARDINESS: Zones 4-8; due to the large range in hardiness, it is best to select a local ecotype
FORM/SHAPE: Upright, oval to round
GROWTH RATE: Slow to moderate
SOIL: Tolerates a range of soils, but performs best in a well-drained, moist, slightly acidic, humus rich soil; does not tolerate wet sites
LIGHT REQUIREMENTS: Full sun to part shade; best growth and color in full sun
DISEASE PROBLEMS: Anthracnose, canker rot, leaf blight, nematodes, powdery mildew, and *Verticillium* wilt
INSECT PROBLEMS: Mapleworm, caterpillars, bagworm, leaf miner, mites, mealybugs, scale, aphids, and thrips
LANDSCAPE VALUE: Large shade tree, excellent fall color
PRUNING TIME: Late winter - early spring
CULTIVARS: Green Mountain® - dark green leaves in summer; fall color is orange to scarlet; 'Legacy' – yellow to orange fall color, drought tolerant; 'Commemoration' – orange to orange-red fall color, fast grower

Alnus serrulata - Hazel Alder, Tag Alder

Alder is a shoreline and wetland tree that has the ability to fix nitrogen due to a relationship with actinomycetes on the roots. This helps it to tolerate poor soils and drought conditions. It is useful for wet areas, shoreline stabilization and wetland mitigation or restoration. Alders provide an excellent wildlife value in the form of food and cover.

PLANT TYPE: Deciduous, broadleaf, small tree
MATURE SIZE: 10-20' in height and 6-12' in width
LEAVES: Alternate, simple, ovate or obovate; dark green leaves; leaf margins are serrated
BARK: Shiny gray-brown
FLOWERS: Male catkins that are conspicuous in Feb-March; female strobile
FRUIT: Oval cone shaped fruit bears lustrous nuts
HARDINESS: Zones 4-9; due to the large range in hardiness, it is best to select a local ecotype
FORM/SHAPE: Multi-stemmed, sometimes suckering
GROWTH RATE: Moderate to fast
SOIL: Tolerates a range of soils, but performs best in a well-drained, moist, slightly acidic soil; likes alluvial soils; tolerates wet sites
LIGHT REQUIREMENTS: Full sun to part shade
DISEASE PROBLEMS: Powdery mildew, gall, and canker
INSECT PROBLEMS: Aphids, lace bug, leaf miner, borers, and occasionally tent caterpillar
LANDSCAPE VALUE: Wet areas, buffers, shoreline/stream-bank stabilization and wetland mitigation/remediation
PRUNING TIME: Late winter – early spring
CULTIVARS: N/A

Amelanchier arborea - Downy Serviceberry

    This is a wonderful tree that offers attractive branching structure, white spring flowers, and fall leaf colors of yellow, orange, or dull red. It can be used as an accent or specimen and is ideal for framing driveways or houses. This is an outstanding tree for woodland gardens, naturalizing, or blending traditional landscapes with surrounding natural areas. Serviceberry is an excellent substitute for Bradford Pear or Florida Dogwood. Also, its fruit, which is a pome and not a berry, possesses great wildlife value. Prune to remove overcrowded or crossing branches.

PLANT TYPE: Deciduous, broadleaf, multi-stemmed, small tree
MATURE SIZE: 15-20' in height, variable spread
LEAVES: Alternate, simple, usually obovate, sometimes elliptic or oblong; young leaves grayish and pubescent changing to dark green in summer; fall color yellow, orange, or dull red
BARK: Grayish and smooth
FLOWERS: White; bloom early to late spring
FRUIT: Round pome, edible
HARDINESS: Zones 4-9; due to the large range in hardiness, it is best to select a local ecotype
FORM/SHAPE: Multi-stemmed, small tree, rounded crown
GROWTH RATE: Moderate
SOIL: Tolerates a range of soils, but performs best in a well-drained, moist, acidic soil
LIGHT REQUIREMENTS: Full sun to part shade
DISEASE PROBLEMS: Cedar serviceberry rust, leaf blight, powdery mildew, Witches' Broom and fruit rot
INSECT PROBLEMS: Aphids, borers, leaf miner, and scales
LANDSCAPE VALUE: Accent tree, specimen planting, woodland gardens, naturalizing, and buffers
PRUNING TIME: Late winter – early spring
CULTIVARS: 'Cole's Select' – this is actually Amelanchier x grandiflora, and has an upright habit with orange—red fall color

Betula nigra - River Birch

This is an extremely versatile tree that is magnificent as a specimen or in groupings. Mature trees offer aesthetic interest in winter because of the light colored papery bark that exfoliates and gives the trees a showy appearance. Multi stemmed individuals are exceptionally nice; three trunks is usually best. Unlike many trees, River Birches do not produce messy fruit drop. In addition to its value in the landscape, it has proven useful for stream bank restoration and wetland mitigation. River Birch prospers in moist or even wet soils, however it can tolerate dry or drought conditions.

PLANT TYPE: Deciduous, broadleaf, large tree
MATURE SIZE: 40-70' in height and 30-50' in width
LEAVES: Alternate, simple, ovate or elliptic; medium to dark green leaves in summer turn yellow in fall; leaf margins are serrated
BARK: Cream colored and smooth in youth; bark exfoliates gray brown to tan papery sheets at maturity
FLOWERS: Male slender dark brown catkins 2-4" long, female oblong to 2cm;
bloom late winter to early spring
FRUIT: Nutlet
HARDINESS: Zones 4-9; due to the large range in hardiness, it is best to select a local ecotype
FORM/SHAPE: Upright, pyramidal in youth, open oval at maturity, can be multi or single-stemmed
GROWTH RATE: Moderate to fast
SOIL: Tolerates a range of soils, but performs best in a well-drained, moist, fertile, humus rich soil; will survive drier sites, but prefers ample moisture; tolerates wet sites
LIGHT REQUIREMENTS: Full sun to part shade
DISEASE PROBLEMS: Anthracnose, canker, leaf blotch, powdery mildew, and *Taphrina* leaf blister
INSECT PROBLEMS: Several borer species, Japanese beetle, aphids, leaf miner, leaf gall aphid, and caterpillars
LANDSCAPE VALUE: Specimen tree, wet areas, buffers, shoreline/stream-bank restoration, and wetland mitigation/remediation
PRUNING TIME: Late winter – early spring
CULTIVARS: Dura-Heat® - compact limb structure and reduced leaf drop during summer droughts; Heritage®- large northern selection

Carpinus caroliniana - American Hornbeam

This tree is usually found in low woods and near streams, but could prove useful in a woodland garden. It is great for naturalizing, blending traditional landscapes with surrounding natural areas, and wet areas. It provides wildlife value in the form of food and cover. As you can see in the picture below, these trees have interesting trunks and bark.

PLANT TYPE: Deciduous, broadleaf, small, sub-canopy tree
MATURE SIZE: 20-30' in height and 15-25' in width
LEAVES: Alternate, simple, elliptic to ovate; dark green leaves; leaf margins are doubly serrate; yellow, orange, or reddish purple in fall
BARK: Smooth, bluish gray, fluted with smooth longitudinal ridges
FLOWERS: Inconspicuous, bloom in spring
FRUIT: Nutlet
HARDINESS: Zones 3-9; due to the large range in hardiness, it is best to select a local ecotype
FORM/SHAPE: Multi-stemmed, bushy shrub or single stemmed tree with a wide spreading crown
GROWTH RATE: Slow to moderate, grows faster in consistently moist soils
SOIL: Well-drained, moist, fertile, humus rich soil; likes alluvial soils; tolerates wet sites
LIGHT REQUIREMENTS: Sun or shade
DISEASE PROBLEMS: Trunk cankers, anthracnose, and leaf spot
INSECT PROBLEMS: Japanese beetle, lace bug, and two-lined chestnut borer
LANDSCAPE VALUE: Naturalizing, wet areas, buffers, and specimen tree
PRUNING TIME: Light pruning in early spring; heavy pruning in winter
CULTIVARS: Palisade® - columnar form

Cercis canadensis - Eastern Redbud

  This bright purple flowering tree can be used as a specimen or in groupings, woodland gardens, and for naturalizing. Its tolerance to many soil types, textures, and pH levels makes it an easy tree to grow. It needs to be pruned for stronger structure and to thin out inner branches that are crossing, crowded, or shaded. Red Buds exhibit moderate drought tolerance, and there are several cultivars that offer variations such as white flowers or purple leaves. There is even a weeping selection available.

PLANT TYPE: Deciduous, broadleaf, small tree
MATURE SIZE: 20-30' in height by 20-30' in width
LEAVES: Alternate, simple, entire, broad-ovate to heart-shaped, palmately veined, medium to dark green
BARK: Smooth, black or brownish black
FLOWERS: Purple to pink, sometimes white; bloom early spring before leaves emerge
FRUIT: Flat legume (pod) appears in fall, greenish turning to brown with maturity
HARDINESS: Zones 4-9; due to the large range in hardiness, it is best to select a local ecotype
FORM/SHAPE: Upright, spreading with rounded or flat crown
GROWTH RATE: Moderate to fast
SOIL: Tolerant to many soil types, textures, and pH levels
LIGHT REQUIREMENTS: Full sun to part shade
DISEASE PROBLEMS: Anthracnose, canker, leaf spot, *Verticillium* wilt
INSECT PROBLEMS: Caterpillar, scale, leaf hopper, red headed Ash borer
LANDSCAPE VALUE: Specimen, groupings, woodland gardens, and naturalizing
PRUNING TIME: Early spring
CULTIVARS: 'Covey' – weeping form; 'Forest Pansy' – purple leaf type; 'Royal White' – white flowered selection

Chionanthus virginicus - Grancy Gray-beard

This plant is a beautiful specimen and provides an excellent food source for wildlife. It also works in groupings and borders, and it can be used for naturalizing as well. Because this species comes in male and female plants (dioecious), female plants require a male for pollination and fruit set. When used as an ornamental, it is best to have males only because their flowers are showy and they lack the messy fruit drop. For naturalizing, a nice mixture of male and female individuals is ideal. Grancy Gray –beard is tough and tolerant to various soil types, textures, and moisture levels. It is a drought tolerant and low maintenance plant.

PLANT TYPE: Deciduous, broadleaf, small tree
MATURE SIZE: 10-18' in height by 6-10' in width
LEAVES: Opposite, simple, narrow elliptic: green leaves turn dull yellow in fall
BARK: Gray, smooth on younger trees, slightly ridged and furrowed on mature trees
FLOWERS: White, slightly fragrant, showy flowers borne on panicles in April to May
FRUIT: Dark blue oval shaped drupe
HARDINESS: Zones 5-9; due to the large range in hardiness, it is best to select a local ecotype
FORM/SHAPE: Upright, open, sometimes wider than high
GROWTH RATE: Slow
SOIL: Extremely adaptable, but prefers a deep, moist, fertile, slightly acidic soil
LIGHT REQUIREMENTS: Full sun to part shade; flowering is best in full sun
DISEASE PROBLEMS: Canker, powdery mildew
INSECT PROBLEMS: None serious, but scale and borer can be a problem
LANDSCAPE VALUE: Specimen, groupings, borders, naturalizing
PRUNING TIME: Late winter – early spring (after flowering)
CULTIVARS: Mostly sold as the species

Cornus florida - Flowering Dogwood

Although this tree exhibits both spring and fall beauty, it comes with an increasing amount of disease and insect problems and is becoming less desirable in the industry. This is a heartbreaking fact because this tree has many uses in the landscape and natural areas, and puts on a spring display of white like no other tree. The part of the inflorescence that most people refer to as the "flower" is actually the 4 white bracts, and the true flowers are inconspicuous, greenish yellow, and found in the middle of the four bracts. There are several cultivars that are resistant to disease. Downy Serviceberry is a good substitute for this tree.

PLANT TYPE: Deciduous, broadleaf, small tree
MATURE SIZE: 20-30' in height and 20-25' in width
LEAVES: Opposite, simple, ovate; medium green leaves turn red to purple in fall
BARK: Smooth, reddish stems when young, older bark consists of square and rectangular grayish blocks
FLOWERS: Yellowish green cluster of true flowers accompanied by four showy white bracts; flowers occur in April
FRUIT: Red drupes
HARDINESS: Zones 5-9; due to the large range in hardiness, it is best to select a local ecotype
FORM/SHAPE: Single or multi-stemmed, usually spreading habit
GROWTH RATE: Moderate
SOIL: Well drained, moist, fertile, humus rich, slightly acidic soil; supplement with micro-nutrients for optimal growth
LIGHT REQUIREMENTS: Part shade, full sun is acceptable with ample moisture
DISEASE PROBLEMS: Anthracnose, Dogwood canker, leaf scorch, *Phytophthora* root rot, leaf blight, and powdery mildew
INSECT PROBLEMS: Dogwood borer, aphids, leaf miner, caterpillars, mealybugs, whiteflies, scales, and several borer species
LANDSCAPE VALUE: Specimen, corners of large buildings or homes, woodland gardens, shoreline/stream-bank restoration, and naturalizing
PRUNING TIME: Rarely needed, spring is the time
CULTIVARS: There are more than 75 cultivars; the following are a few that possess disease resistance. 'Cherokee Brave' – dark pink flowers, good resistance to powdery mildew; 'Junior Miss' – large flowered; some resistance to anthracnose and canker; 'Stella Pink' – pink flowers, some resistance to powdery mildew

Diospyros virginiana - Common Persimmon

Persimmon is a tough tree that can tolerate poor fertility and dry conditions. It is great for naturalizing, mitigation, and habitiat enhancement. This tree offers a valuable food source to many species of wildlife. It can also be eaten by humans, but be sure to wait until the first frost of the year to ensure a nice sweet fruit. If eaten too early the bitterness will turn you mouth inside out.

PLANT TYPE: Deciduous, broadleaf, medium tree
MATURE SIZE: 40-70' in height and 20-35' in width
LEAVES: Alternate, simple, ovate to elliptic or widely lance shape, dark green, lustrous; turn reddish in fall
STEM/BARK: Young stems grayish brown; trunk is dark gray almost black, thick square scales
FLOWERS: White to greenish white; male and female flowers are usually on separate individuals (dioecious), female flowers usually solitary and males clustered; appear May-June
FRUIT: Pale orange, fleshy berry ripens in fall
HARDINESS: Zones 4-9; due to the large range in hardiness, it is best to select a local ecotype
FORM/SHAPE: Oval crown and usually symmetric in shape
GROWTH RATE: Slow
SOIL: Tolerant to soil texture and pH; prefers moist, fertile, well-drained, sandy loam
LIGHT REQUIREMENTS: Full sun
DISEASE PROBLEMS: Powdery mildew, fungal leaf spots, blight
INSECT PROBLEMS: Fall webworm and tent caterpillars
LANDSCAPE VALUE: Naturalizing, mitigation, and wildlife habitat
PRUNING TIME: Late winter
CULTIVARS: Not common

Fagus grandifolia - American Beech

This is a beautiful tree with excellent wildlife value. American Beech is usually a more vigorous grower in the United States than the European Beech, and it is one of the dominant species in old growth and climax forests. It prefers the cooler north and northeast facing slopes. If given ample moisture, this is a great shade, specimen, or park tree, and it is useful for naturalizing and mitigation. The light gray bark is very smooth and beautiful, but please don't carve into it.

PLANT TYPE: Deciduous, broadleaf, large tree
MATURE SIZE: 50-100' in height and 40-70' in width
LEAVES: Alternate, simple, ovate-oblong, dark green leaves with distinct veins and serrate margins; fall color is bronze; many times the leaves will remain on the tree throughout the winter
BARK: Thin, smooth, gray with darker mottling
FLOWERS: Inconspicuous, flowers occur in spring
FRUIT: Brown, three-winged edible nut held in a prickly, dehiscent husk (involucre)
HARDINESS: Zones 3-8 (some literature claims 4-9); due to the large range in hardiness, it is best to select a local ecotype
FORM/SHAPE: Upright with a wide-spreading crown
GROWTH RATE: Slow to moderate
SOIL: Moist, fertile, well-drained, acidic soil
LIGHT REQUIREMENTS: Full sun to part shade, best growth in full sun
DISEASE PROBLEMS: Bleeding canker, powdery mildew, leaf spots, cankers, root rot, and wood decay
INSECT PROBLEMS: Aphids, caterpillars, leaf miner, Beech scale, Beech lacebug, Beech mealybug, locust, leafhopper, galling insects, and several borer species
LANDSCAPE VALUE: Large areas, shade tree, specimen, park tree, mitigation, and naturalizing
PRUNING TIME: Rarely needed, late winter – early spring
CULTIVARS: N/A

Fraxinus pennsylvanica - Green Ash

Green Ash is a shoreline or wetland tree that is tolerant of drought, salt, and poor air quality; therefore it has an array of uses. It is an ideal shade tree or street tree, and can be used for parks, golf courses, or wetland mitigation. Although it lacks showy flowers and fall leaf color, it is a fast growing, tough, and versatile tree.

PLANT TYPE: Deciduous, broadleaf, large tree
MATURE SIZE: 50-60' in height and 25-35' in width
LEAVES: Opposite, pinnately compound, 5 to 11 leaflets, dark green and turn yellow in fall
BARK: Smooth, gray to gray-brown with diamond shaped furrows separated by narrow ridges
FLOWERS: Inconspicuous, flowers occur in spring
FRUIT: Samara
HARDINESS: Zones 2-9, due to the large range in hardiness, it is best to select a local ecotype
FORM/SHAPE: Upright, oval crown
GROWTH RATE: Fast
SOIL: Tolerant of any soil condition, does best in a moist, deep soil
LIGHT REQUIREMENTS: Full sun to part shade, best growth in full sun
DISEASE PROBLEMS: Ash dieback, Ash yellows, leaf rusts, cankers, and leaf spots
INSECT PROBLEMS: Ash borer, several other borer species, tent caterpillars, carpenter worm, gall midge, leaf miner, Ash sawfly, and several scale species
LANDSCAPE VALUE: Shade tree, street tree, parks, golf courses, and wetland mitigation/remediation
PRUNING TIME: Late winter – early spring
CULTIVARS: 'Patmore' – Hardy in Zones 2-8; uniform habit; Urbanite® - pyramidal form, dark green leaves with bronze fall color; seedless

Halesia carolina - Carolina Silverbell

Carolina Silverbell is a beautiful tree that produces many white flowers in the spring. It also has an attractive bark and is a very low maintenance plant. Its many uses include woodland gardens, specimens, naturalizing, wetland mitigation, and stream bank restoration. Rhododendrons and Azaleas grow well under these trees, and they make a great woodland garden focal point.

PLANT TYPE: Deciduous, broadleaf, medium tree
MATURE SIZE: 30-40' in height and 25-35' in width
LEAVES: Alternate, simple, ovate or elliptic, green turning yellow in fall
BARK: Gray to brown with ridges that develop into scaly plates
FLOWERS: White, bell shaped, borne on long pendulous stalks in axillary clusters; flowering occurs in spring
FRUIT: Four-winged, dry drupe
HARDINESS: Zones 5-8
FORM/SHAPE: Low branched tree with a broad rounded crown
GROWTH RATE: Moderate to fast
SOIL: Moist, well-drained, acidic, and highly organic soil
LIGHT REQUIREMENTS: Full sun to part shade, best growth in full sun
DISEASE PROBLEMS: None serious
INSECT PROBLEMS: None serious
LANDSCAPE VALUE: Woodland gardens, specimen tree, naturalizing, wetland mitigation/remediation, and stream bank restoration
PRUNING TIME: Late winter – early spring
CULTIVARS: 'Arnold Pink' – rose pink flowers; 'Wedding Bells' – large white flowers

Hamamelis virginiana - Common Witchhazel

This small tree offers yellow flowers in the late fall or early winter months when not much is happening in the landscapes and woodlands. This is a nice tree to add interest to the garden or enhance moist woodlands. The seeds are a food source for turkey and bobwhite. This tree requires ample moisture, but is relatively insect and disease free.

PLANT TYPE: Deciduous, broadleaf, small tree
MATURE SIZE: 15-20' in height and 10-15' in width
LEAVES: Alternate, ovate, obovate, or elliptic, green turning yellow in fall
BARK: Gray to gray-brown
FLOWERS: Yellow, fragrant, spider-like flowers borne on 2-4 flowered cymes that occur in fall to winter
FRUIT: Pubescent capsule containing 4 shiny brown seeds
HARDINESS: Zones 3-8, due to the large range in hardiness, it is best to select a local ecotype
FORM/SHAPE: Irregular, rounded, open branch structure
GROWTH RATE: Moderate
SOIL: Moist, well-drained, acidic, and highly organic soil; will tolerate heavy clay
LIGHT REQUIREMENTS: Full sun to part shade, best growth, flowering, and leaf color occurs in full sun
DISEASE PROBLEMS: None serious
INSECT PROBLEMS: None serious
LANDSCAPE VALUE: Small specimen tree, woodland gardens, and naturalizing
PRUNING TIME: Minimal pruning in late winter to early spring
CULTIVARS: N/A

Ilex opaca - American Holly

This is one of the few native plants that are evergreen, and it offers brilliant red fruits during the fall and winter. In addition to their beauty, the fruits offer a food source to many birds and small mammals. These trees tolerate a wide variety of soil conditions. I've seen individuals growing in low flat areas near a creek and then find them growing on dry upland slopes. American Holly is extremely drought tolerant, but is not tolerant of high winds.

PLANT TYPE: Evergreen, broadleaf, medium tree
MATURE SIZE: 15-30' in height and 10-20' in width; some reach 40-50' in height
LEAVES: Alternate, simple, elliptic with large spines, dark green
BARK: Smooth, light gray; turns dark gray with age
FLOWERS: Male flowers are in cymes, female flowers are 1-3 on a peduncle, greenish white, fragrant; flowering occurs April-May
FRUIT: Round, red drupe that matures in fall and persists through winter
HARDINESS: Zones 5-9, due to the large range in hardiness, it is best to select a local ecotype
FORM/SHAPE: Columnar or conical with branches to the ground
GROWTH RATE: Slow to moderate
SOIL: Moist, well-drained, acid soil
LIGHT REQUIREMENTS: Part sun to full sun
DISEASE PROBLEMS: Leaf spots, leaf drop, powdery mildew, cankers, twig dieback, spot anthracnose
INSECT PROBLEMS: Leaf miner, scale, berry midge, southern red mite
LANDSCAPE VALUE: Specimen, grouping, xeriscapes, mitigation, and naturalizing
PRUNING TIME: Late winter
CULTIVARS: 'Croonenburg' – compact, pyramidal tree with wavy leaves and less spines than the species; fruits heavily; 'Greenleaf' – pyramidal tree with glossy green, spiny leaves, bright red fruits

Juniperus virginiana - Eastern Red Cedar

This is another one of the few native plants that is evergreen. It can be used as a specimen, screen, grouping, windbreak, large hedge, xeriscape tree, and for naturalizing. It exhibits good drought tolerance and provides excellent wildlife value in the form of food and cover.

PLANT TYPE: Evergreen, coniferous, large tree
MATURE SIZE: 30-50' in height and 10-20' in width
LEAVES: Opposite, scale like leaves in a whorled arrangement; medium to dark green foliage turns to bronze or purple in winter
BARK: Rough, gray to reddish brown; exfoliating in long fibers or strips
FLOWERS: During winter, male trees bear yellowish cones; female trees bear greenish to blue green cones that result in an attractive display
FRUIT: Fleshy, drupe-like, globular, cone, blue to purple
HARDINESS: Zones 3-8, due to the large range in hardiness, it is best to select a local ecotype
FORM/SHAPE: Pyramidal in youth; irregular oval with age
GROWTH RATE: Moderate
SOIL: Extremely tolerant to a wide range of soil types, textures, and pH values; prefers a moist, well-drained, well-limed soil
LIGHT REQUIREMENTS: Full sun
DISEASE PROBLEMS: Cedar apple rust, Juniper blight
INSECT PROBLEMS: Spider mites, bagworm
LANDSCAPE VALUE: Specimen, screen, grouping, windbreak, large hedge, xeriscapes, and naturalizing
PRUNING TIME: Little to none needed
CULTIVARS: 'Burkii' – narrow pyramidal, 15-25 feet in height; 'Globosa' – compact form, less height and more density than the species

Liquidambar styraciflua – Sweetgum

This is another one of those trees that offers a nice display of fall leaf color, and it is quite a tough tree whose uses include lawn tree, street tree, park tree, naturalizing, or wetland mitigation. The fruit drop from this tree is messy; therefore it is best to use fruitless cultivars in the landscape.

PLANT TYPE: Deciduous, broadleaf, large tree
MATURE SIZE: 60-80' in height and 35-45' in width
LEAVES: Alternate, simple, 5-7 acute lobed, star-shaped with finely serrate margins; dark green turning yellow, orange, or red in fall
BARK: Smooth, light gray when young; dark gray with rough, narrow ridges and furrows when mature; twigs have corky wings
FLOWERS: Not showy, greenish, flowering occurs in April-May
FRUIT: Hard, spiny green ball (syncarp of dehiscent capsules), turns brown in fall
HARDINESS: Zones 5-9, due to the large range in hardiness, it is best to select a local ecotype
FORM/SHAPE: Pyramidal
GROWTH RATE: Moderate to fast
SOIL: Tolerant of various soil conditions, but prefers a well-drained, moist, slightly acidic soil; tolerates wet conditions and short periods of inundation
LIGHT REQUIREMENTS: Full sun to part shade, best growth and color in full sun
DISEASE PROBLEMS: Bleeding canker, leaf spot, and root rot
INSECT PROBLEMS: Tent caterpillar, cottony-cushion scale, sweetgum scale, and aphids
LANDSCAPE VALUE: Lawn tree, parks, street tree, naturalizing, or wetland mitigation/remediation
PRUNING TIME: Minimal pruning; if done winter is best time
CULTIVARS: Cherokee® - fruitless for the most part, vigorous grower, fall color burgundy to red; 'Rotundiloba' – leaf lobes are rounded rather than acute, various fall color ranges from yellow to burgundy, sets no fruit

Liriodendron tulipifera - Tulip Poplar

Tulip Poplar is a member of the Magnolia family and is good for use in large areas as a shade tree, specimen, or for naturalizing. Its extremely nice flowers can often be overlooked because they are so high up in the air, but if you look up closely you can admire their beauty. The fall color is an intense golden yellow and comes earlier than most trees. Restrict the use of this tree to large areas because the wood can be weak in some individuals.

PLANT TYPE: Deciduous, broadleaf, large tree
MATURE SIZE: 70-100' in height and 35-50' in width
LEAVES: Alternate, simple, large, broad spatulate, 4-6 lobes; green to dark green leaves turn yellow in fall
BARK: Grayish brown to gray; mature trees develop deep crevices and large flat ridges
FLOWERS: Greenish yellow with orange markings at the base of the petals; there are 6 petals on the solitary flowers that bloom in late spring after the leaves emerge
FRUIT: Aggregate of samaras
HARDINESS: Zones 4-9, due to the large range in hardiness, it is best to select a local ecotype
FORM/SHAPE: Symmetric, pyramidal in youth, becomes oval crowned with age; in a forest situation the tree has a tall trunk with a narrow conical crown formed by branches on the upper reaches of the tree; only 20-30% of the tree consists of branches
GROWTH RATE: Fast
SOIL: Well-drained, moist, fertile soil, pH adaptable, prefers slightly acidic soil
LIGHT REQUIREMENTS: Full sun
DISEASE PROBLEMS: Bark rot, canker, dieback, leaf spots, powdery mildew, root rot, and *Verticillium* wilt
INSECT PROBLEMS: Yellow poplar weevil, caterpillars, scale, and aphids, which are a major problem
LANDSCAPE VALUE: Use in large areas as shade tree or specimen, and for naturalizing
PRUNING TIME: Winter, although rarely needed
CULTIVARS: 'Aureomarginatum' – green leaves with yellow to yellow-green margin; 'Fastigiatum' – narrow, lateral branches grow upright, 50-60' tall and 15-20' wide

Magnolia grandiflora - Southern Magnolia

This evergreen tree is a southeastern classic that produces a large, fragrant white flower in spring and summer. Southern Magnolia is tough and relatively free of disease and insects. It is excellent as a specimen, screen or hedge. Smaller cultivars can be used on large corners of houses or buildings. These trees have proven useful in xeriscapes and for naturalizing. There are many cultivars that offer various sizes, forms, and leaf types. It offers food and cover to many bird species.

PLANT TYPE: Evergreen, broadleaf, large tree
MATURE SIZE: 60-80' in height and 30-50' in width
LEAVES: Alternate, simple, elliptic, lustrous dark green, glabrous (smooth) above and usually pubescent beneath
BARK: Smooth and gray
FLOWERS: Large, showy, and fragrant; solitary, 8-12" and bloom in May-June, longer for some cultivars
FRUIT: Scarlet seeds on a cone like structure that is actually an aggregate of follicles
HARDINESS: Zones 7-9
FORM/SHAPE: Pyramidal, low-branching, sometimes branches go all the way to the ground
GROWTH RATE: Slow to moderate
SOIL: Well-drained, moist, fertile soil
LIGHT REQUIREMENTS: Full sun to part shade
DISEASE PROBLEMS: Relatively disease free
INSECT PROBLEMS: Relatively insect free, but can get Magnolia scale as well as several other types of scale and leaf miner
LANDSCAPE VALUE: Specimen tree, screen or hedge, xeriscapes, and naturalizing
PRUNING TIME: Early spring
CULTIVARS: 'Bracken's Brown Beauty' – smaller and more dense than the species and with smaller leaves and flowers; leaves with wavy margins and heavily pubescent underneath; 'Claudia Wannamaker'– broadly pyramidal, large selection (40-50') flowers at early age; 'Little Gem' – one of the smallest forms available; flowers occurring May-June and continue into late fall

Nyssa sylvatica - Black Gum

This tree exhibits wonderful fall color, and its fruit is a food source for many species of birds and small mammals. It can be used as a specimen or in buffers as well as for naturalizing and wetland mitigation. This species has two naturally occurring varieties: sylvatica, which is found in dry ecosystems and biflora, which is found in moist to wet ecosystems. This plant, especially the sylvatica variety, is drought tolerant.

PLANT TYPE: Deciduous, broadleaf, large tree
MATURE SIZE: 30-65' in height and 20-35' in width
LEAVES: Alternate, simple, obovate or elliptic, entire green leaves that turn a brilliant red (sometimes deep purple) in the fall
BARK: Smooth and dark gray when young; dark gray or brown-black with deep ridges broken into block-like segments at maturity
FLOWERS: Inconspicuous, emerge in spring with leaves
FRUIT: Dark blue, oval shaped drupe
HARDINESS: Zones 4-9, due to the large range in hardiness, it is best to select a local ecotype
FORM/SHAPE: Pyramidal to oval, usually symmetric
GROWTH RATE: Slow to moderate
SOIL: Moist, well-drained, slightly acidic soil; tolerant to many different soil textures
LIGHT REQUIREMENTS: Full sun to part shade; plant growth and fall color is best in sun
DISEASE PROBLEMS: Cankers and leaf spot
INSECT PROBLEMS: Scales, tent caterpillars, and Tupelo leaf miner
LANDSCAPE VALUE: Specimen tree, naturalizing, buffer strips, and wetland mitigation/remediation
PRUNING TIME: Late winter – early spring
CULTIVARS: N/A

Ostrya virginiana - American Hophornbeam

This is a versatile tree that is ideal for naturalizing yet, performs well in city landscapes. It has no serious threat for disease or insects and is moderately tolerant to drought. It is often used as a lawn tree or a park tree in the landscape. The bark is a spectacular display of nature.

PLANT TYPE: Deciduous, broadleaf, medium tree
MATURE SIZE: 20-40' in height and 20-30' in width
LEAVES: Alternate, simple, ovate to elliptic, serrate, dark green
STEM/BARK: Grayish brown and shredding
FLOWERS: Male catkin, yellow, about 2" appear in late winter; female catkins with paired flowers 2-3 cm long appear in April
FRUIT: Clusters of ovoid nuts or nutlets
HARDINESS: Zones 4-9, due to the large range in hardiness, it is best to select a local ecotype
FORM/SHAPE: Conical tree becoming more fanned out with age
GROWTH RATE: Slow
SOIL: Moist, well drained, slightly acidic
LIGHT REQUIREMENTS: Sun to part shade
DISEASE PROBLEMS: None serious
INSECT PROBLEMS: None serious
LANDSCAPE VALUE: Lawn tree, park tree, naturalizing
PRUNING TIME: Late Winter
CULTIVARS: N/A

Oxydendrum arboreum - Sourwood

Sourwood trees are interesting under story trees that are made famous by the well known and sought after Sourwood Honey. It is a beautiful tree with interest in all seasons. It offers a white tassel like inflorescence of flowers in the summer, intense red fall leaf color, and has quite an interesting display of bark. It is not good for urban use, but makes a spectacular specimen tree in landscapes and natural areas.

PLANT TYPE: Deciduous, broadleaf, medium, usually a sub - canopy tree
MATURE SIZE: 30-60' (usually on the smaller end of this range) in height and 20-25' in width
LEAVES: Alternate, simple, lanceolate to elliptic-lanceolate, dark green turn to bright red or orange in fall
BARK: Grayish brown, thick with deep fissures and ridges once mature
FLOWERS: White, terminal clusters of racemes with urn-shaped flowers that appear in early summer
FRUIT: Dehiscent, oval-shaped capsule, persistant
HARDINESS: Zones 5-9, due to the large range in hardiness, it is best to select a local ecotype
FORM/SHAPE: Pyramidal crown with branches that droop, usually the tree or some of its branches are irregular and leaning when found in the wild
GROWTH RATE: Slow to moderate
SOIL: Moist, well-drained, humus rich, slightly acidic soil
LIGHT REQUIREMENTS: Full sun to part shade, flowers and fall color best in full sun
DISEASE PROBLEMS: None serious; canker, leaf spot and twig blight are possible
INSECT PROBLEMS: Several species of stem borers
LANDSCAPE VALUE: Specimen or naturalizing
PRUNING TIME: Minimal pruning required; late winter if at all
CULTIVARS: Rare

Pinus strobus - Eastern White Pine

This evergreen tree offers beautiful blue green foliage, and nice branching structure. It is used as a specimen, park tree, hedge, or screen, and it is useful for mitigation, and naturalizing. It is one of the few pines that can be used as a hedge, and it is a good source of food and cover for small birds.

PLANT TYPE: Evergreen, coniferous, large tree
MATURE SIZE: 50-80' in height and 30-40' in width
LEAVES: Five needles per fascicle, blue-green, spiraled arrangement
BARK: Gray and smooth when young, becomes thick rectangular blocked when mature
FLOWERS: Monoecious, males are in clusters, and are yellow in color (heavy pollen production); females are pinkish
FRUIT: Slender cones, greenish cone turns brown with maturity
HARDINESS: Zones 3-7, due to the large range in hardiness, it is best to select a local ecotype
FORM/SHAPE: Symmetrical when young, matures to and irregular spreading form with age
GROWTH RATE: Fast
SOIL: Moist, well-drained, slightly acidic soil; does not tolerate heavy clay; can tolerate a range of moisture levels from extremely dry to boggy
LIGHT REQUIREMENTS: Part shade to full sun; mature trees need full sun
DISEASE PROBLEMS: White Pine blister rust, canker, needle blight, needle rust, and gall
INSECT PROBLEMS: White Pine weevil, Southern Pine beetle, bagworm, and Pine spittlebug
LANDSCAPE VALUE: Specimen, park tree, hedge, screen, mitigation, and naturalizing
PRUNING TIME: None needed except to remove dead limbs
CULTIVARS: 'Pendula' – weeping type; 'Prostrata' – dwarf type 8-10' in height

Platanus occidentalis – Sycamore

Sycamore is a large majestic tree that can be used in the landscape, but it is best utilized in natural areas. This tree tolerates many soil types and is adapted to wet soils, periodic flooding and moderate drought. These traits make it a great native tree for wetland, stream-bank, and shoreline plantings.

PLANT TYPE: Deciduous, broadleaf, large tree
MATURE SIZE: 75-100' in height and the same or greater in width
LEAVES: Alternate, simple, broad leaf; 3-5 triangular lobes, light green leaves turn pale yellow in fall
BARK: Gray brown sometimes with a reddish tint; exfoliating on upper trunk exposing whitish colored bark
FLOWERS: Male and female flowers are brownish globose (ball-like) structures
FRUIT: Ball shaped grouping of achenes (multiple fruit)
HARDINESS: Zones 4-9, due to the large range in hardiness, it is best to select a local ecotype
FORM/SHAPE: Pyramidal in youth, becoming massive, spreading and irregular with maturity
GROWTH RATE: Moderate to fast
SOIL: Tolerant of just about any soil type, but prefers a deep, fertile, moist, well-drained soil; tolerates short periods of inundation
LIGHT REQUIREMENTS: Full sun to light shade
DISEASE PROBLEMS: Anthracnose, powdery mildew, and canker
INSECT PROBLEMS: Mealybugs, aphids, mites, Japanese beetle, Sycamore lacebug, cottony Maple scale, and several borers
LANDSCAPE VALUE: Not an ideal landscape choice due to the dropping of leaves, branches, and fruits; best used for naturalizing, buffers, wetland mitigation/remediation, shorelines, and stream-banks
PRUNING TIME: Winter

CULTIVARS: Some hybrids available (*Platanus x acerifolia*)

Quercus alba - White Oak

White Oaks are one of the primary trees in old growth or climax forests. When found in the forest competing with other trees they are tall, narrow, and irregular in shape, but out in the open as a shade tree or specimen they are wide and nicely rounded. They provide wildlife with food (acorns) during the crucial late fall and winter months when all other food sources become less or non available. White Oaks are utilized by ducks, quail, several species of songbirds, and are of great importance to Deer and Turkey.

PLANT TYPE: Deciduous, broadleaf, large tree
MATURE SIZE: 50-100' in height, and 50-80' in width
LEAVES: Alternate, simple, oblong-ovate with 7-9 deep, rounded lobes; green leaves turn brown (sometimes purplish) in fall
BARK: Gray, with deep furrows, scaly or flaky
FLOWERS: Yellowish brown, appear in early spring
FRUIT: Acorn, brown, ½ -1" long, ovoid, held in a bowl like series of bracts
HARDINESS: Zones 3-8, due to the large range in hardiness, it is best to select a local ecotype
FORM/SHAPE: Pyramidal when young, matures to a rounded crown; can have wide spreading branches particularly when growing in open space.
GROWTH RATE: Moderate
SOIL: Tolerates a wide range of soil types; prefers a deep, moist, well-drained, slightly acidic soil
LIGHT REQUIREMENTS: Full sun to part shade
DISEASE PROBLEMS: Anthracnose, basal canker, canker, powdery mildew, and wood decay
INSECT PROBLEMS: Mites, leaf miner, oak skeletonizer, several species of scales and borers
LANDSCAPE VALUE: Shade tree, lawn tree, mitigation, naturalizing, and habitat enhancement
PRUNING TIME: Late winter to early spring

CULTIVARS: N/A

Quercus coccinea - Scarlet Oak

These trees can be used as shade trees, street trees, or for parking lots, xeriscapes, and naturalizing. Scarlet oaks possess tolerance to drought and pollution. They hold their copper colored leaves throughout the winter and into early spring. Like most Oaks, they are a good food source for birds and mammals.

PLANT TYPE: Deciduous, broadleaf, large tree
MATURE SIZE: 60-70' in height and 40-50' in width
LEAVES: Alternate, simple, deep lobes with bristle tips; green leaves turn to a bright reddish (scarlet) or russet color in fall.
BARK: Smooth; gray, becomes darker with age
FLOWERS: Male and female catkins, female catkins matures to acorn
FRUIT: Hard, brown acorn, ½" by ¾" in size
HARDINESS: Zones 4-9, due to the large range in hardiness, it is best to select a local ecotype
FORM/SHAPE: Pyramidal in open space
GROWTH RATE: Moderate
SOIL: Well-drained moist, fertile, slightly acidic
LIGHT REQUIREMENTS: Full sun
DISEASE PROBLEMS: Anthracnose, cankers, and root rots
INSECT PROBLEMS: Ambrosia beetles, caterpillars, leaf miner, Oak webworm, Oak skeletonizer, and several different borers and scales
LANDSCAPE VALUE: Shade tree, parking lots, street tree, xeriscapes, and naturalizing
PRUNING TIME: Late winter to early spring
CULTIVARS: N/A

Quercus lyrata - Overcup Oak

This tree tolerates infrequent flooding, yet it is moderately tolerant to drought. These characteristics make it useful for shade, parking lots, street trees, wetland mitigation, and naturalizing. Also, it is one of the faster growing Oaks available.

PLANT TYPE: Deciduous, broadleaf, large tree
MATURE SIZE: 30-40' in height and 25-30' in width
LEAVES: Alternate, simple, dark green leaves turn copper in the fall
BARK: Gray-brown with plates or broad ridges
FLOWERS: Brown male catkin, greenish female flower
FRUIT: Acorn, bracts almost cover entire nut; acorns are about 1" in size
HARDINESS: Zones 6-9
FORM/SHAPE: Pyramidal, rounded with maturity
GROWTH RATE: Fast
SOIL: Tolerant to many soils, but prefers a well drained, moist, fertile soil
LIGHT REQUIREMENTS: Full sun
DISEASE PROBLEMS: Canker, root rot
INSECT PROBLEMS: leaf miner, mites, caterpillars, webworms, and several borers
LANDSCAPE VALUE: Shade tree, parking lots, street tree, wetland mitigation/remediation and naturalizing
PRUNING TIME: Late winter to early spring
CULTIVARS: N/A

Quercus palustris - Pin Oak

This is a popular landscape tree and a great tree for wet areas. Moreover, they are tough, versatile, and tolerant to drought. They are easily transplanted due to the shallow fibrous root system. They can be used for shade, parking lots, commercial landscapes, buffer strips, mitigation, xeriscapes, and naturalizing. This is another Oak that holds its leaves throughout winter, and as with many Oaks is a valuable food source to wildlife.

PLANT TYPE: Deciduous, broadleaf, large tree
MATURE SIZE: 50-75' in height and 25-40' in width
LEAVES: Alternate, simple, 5-7 deep lobes; shiny, dark green leaves; turn red or brown in fall
BARK: Gray and smooth when young; dark and fissured into broad scaly ridges when mature
FLOWERS: Greenish to tan male catkin; yellowish female flower; bloom in early spring
FRUIT: Small, round, 1/2'" in size, light brown acorn in a shallow saucer shaped cap (bracts)
HARDINESS: Zones 4-8, due to the large range in hardiness, it is best to select a local ecotype
FORM/SHAPE: Straight-trunk tree with a pyramidal crown
GROWTH RATE: Moderate to fast
SOIL: Prefers moist, rich, well-drained, slightly acidic soil; will tolerate flooding
LIGHT REQUIREMENTS: Full sun
DISEASE PROBLEMS: Galls, canker, and iron chlorosis in soils with high pH
INSECT PROBLEMS: Mites, caterpillars, Oak webworm, and several species of borers
LANDSCAPE VALUE: Shade tree, parking lots, commercial landscapes, buffer strips, mitigation, xeriscapes, and naturalizing
PRUNING TIME: Late winter to early spring to maintain a central leader, remove low hanging limbs, or damaged limbs
CULTIVARS: 'Crown Right' – more upright habit

Quercus phellos - Willow Oak

Willow Oak offers value in the urban landscape as a street or parking lot tree, yet they have their place in the sub urban and rural landscapes. This drought tolerant tree is easily transplanted, tough, and versatile. And like many Oaks, it provides mammals with a valuable food source.

PLANT TYPE: Deciduous, broadleaf, large tree
MATURE SIZE: 50-80' in height and 40-50' in width
LEAVES: Alternate, simple, narrowly oblong or lanceolate
BARK: Dark gray, smooth; becomes blackish, slightly ridged, and furrowed at maturity
FLOWERS: Dull green to tan male catkin; brownish green female flower, bloom in early spring
FRUIT: Small, ½" and oval to nearly round; held in a shallow saucer shape cap (bracts)
HARDINESS: Zones 5-9, due to the large range in hardiness, it is best to select a local ecotype
FORM/SHAPE: Pyramidal in youth, oval to rounded with maturity
GROWTH RATE: Moderate to fast
SOIL: Very tolerant to a wide variety of soils, but prefers a moist, well-drained, fertile, slightly acidic soil
LIGHT REQUIREMENTS: Full sun to part shade
DISEASE PROBLEMS: None serious
INSECT PROBLEMS: Mites, webworms, and several borer species
LANDSCAPE VALUE: Street tree, shade tree, parking lots, commercial landscapes, mitigation, xeriscapes, and naturalizing
PRUNING TIME: Late winter to early spring to maintain a central leader, remove low hanging limbs, or damaged limbs
CULTIVARS: Mostly grown as the species

Quercus prinus - Chestnut Oak

This is an excellent tree for poor, dry, or rocky soil. Unlike many of the Oaks that possess similar leaf shapes, Chestnut Oaks have a distinct leaf. This is a tough tree useful as a specimen, a shade tree, or a roadside planting. Chestnut Oaks are also good trees for naturalizing and habitat enhancement.

PLANT TYPE: Deciduous, broadleaf, large tree
MATURE SIZE: 60-70' in height and 40-50' in width
LEAVES: Alternate, simple, obovate, leaf margin is wavy with 10-16 teeth, lustrous, dark green leaves turn orange-yellow in fall
STEM/BARK: Brownish-gray with conspicuous lenticels, trunk is dark and furrowed
FLOWERS: Catkin
FRUIT: Acorn, dark brown, egg shaped, at least one third covered by cap (bract)
HARDINESS: Zones 4-8, due to the large range in hardiness, it is best to select a local ecotype
FORM/SHAPE: Pyramidal to oval in youth, rounded with age
GROWTH RATE: Moderate
SOIL: Tolerant, prefers moist, well-drained, tolerant to dry, rocky conditions
LIGHT REQUIREMENTS: Full sun to part shade
DISEASE PROBLEMS: Canker, leaf spots, powdery mildew
INSECT PROBLEMS: Insect galls, caterpillar, several species of borers
LANDSCAPE VALUE: Specimen, shade tree, lawn tree, naturalizing, and habitat enhancement
PRUNING TIME: Late winter
CULTIVARS: N/A

Quercus shumardii - Shumard Oak

This is a wonderful tree for its aesthetics, and it is tolerant to poor soils, air pollution, wet or boggy soils, and even dry conditions. Shumard Oak is valuable food source for birds and mammals.

PLANT TYPE: Large, deciduous, broadleaf, tree
MATURE SIZE: 60-80' in height and 40-50' in width
LEAVES: Alternate, simple, obovate or elliptic, 5-9 lobes, lustrous, dark green, turn yellowish or possible a nice red to reddish orange in fall
STEM/BARK: gray brown in youth, gray with ridges and fissures when mature
FLOWERS: Brownish male catkin, greenish female catkin
FRUIT: Acorns
HARDINESS: Zone 5-9, due to the large range in hardiness, it is best to select a local ecotype
FORM/SHAPE: Pyramidal when young, rounded and spreading with age
GROWTH RATE: Moderate to fast
SOIL: moist, well drained, slightly acidic; quite adaptable
LIGHT REQUIREMENTS: Full sun to part sun
DISEASE PROBLEMS: Canker rot, leaf blight
INSECT PROBLEMS: Leaf miner, caterpillars, several species of borers and scales
LANDSCAPE VALUE: Lawn tree, shade tree buffer strips, naturalizing, shoreline and stream-bank, restoration
PRUNING TIME: Late Winter
CULTIVARS: N/A

Quercus virginiana - Live Oak

Live Oaks are one of the few evergreen Oaks found in our forests and landscapes. This is usually a low country or coastal tree, but can be found in the piedmont and foothills as well. These large majestic trees can be used for shade, street trees, parks, golf courses, campuses, habitat enhancement, naturalizing, and mitigation. Salt tolerance of this tree is moderate to high, and the acorns of Live Oaks are a valuable food source for several species of birds and mammals.

PLANT TYPE: Evergreen, broadleaf, large tree
MATURE SIZE: 60-80' in height and 60-120' in width
LEAVES: Alternate, simple, elliptical to obovate, leathery, dark green above, olive green below
BARK: Gray to tan and smooth in youth; matures to a dark gray to blackish gray with rough blocky ridges
FLOWERS: Males in catkins; females 1-5 flowers in axils; bloom early to mid spring
FRUIT: Acorn, ellipsoidal cap covering 1/3 of the dark brown nut
HARDINESS: Zones (7)8-10
FORM/SHAPE: Spreading, wide crown; horizontal, arching, and occasionally curved branches form a broad, rounded crown; forms a massive canopy
GROWTH RATE: Slow to moderate
SOIL: Tolerant to a wide range of soils; will tolerate periodically wet soil
LIGHT REQUIREMENTS: Part sun to full sun
DISEASE PROBLEMS: Several kinds of root rot
INSECT PROBLEMS: Insect gall
LANDSCAPE VALUE: Shade tree, street tree, parks, golf courses, habitat enhancement, naturalizing, and mitigation/restoration
PRUNING TIME: Late winter
CULTIVARS: 'Highrise' – upright pyramidal, possibly even columnar

Sabal palmetto – Cabbage Palmetto, Sabal Palm

This is a wonderful tree for coastal plain and maritime landscapes or ecosystems. It can tolerate periodic inundation, drought, high winds, and exposure to salinity. Fruits eaten by songbirds, bobwhite, small mammals, turkey, deer, and bear.

PLANT TYPE: Evergreen, monocot, large palm tree
MATURE SIZE: 40-50' in height and 12-20' in width
LEAVES: Fan shaped, 3-6' long, dark green; old petioles persistent
STEM/BARK: Gray
FLOWERS: Cream, 3-5' long panicles that bloom in summer
FRUIT: Drupes, green at first then turning black
HARDINESS: Zones 8-11
FORM/SHAPE: Large palm with a dense, round crown
GROWTH RATE: Slow
SOIL: Tolerant to sand, loam, or clay, acidic or alkaline; prefers a moist, fertile, well-drained, loam; tolerates wet or dry conditions once established
LIGHT REQUIREMENTS: Full sun to part shade
DISEASE PROBLEMS: Butt rot, false smut, and tar spot can be a problem
INSECT PROBLEMS: None serious
LANDSCAPE VALUE: Specimen, groupings, medians, roadsides, mitigation, and naturalizing
PRUNING TIME: Remove brown or yellow older leaves as needed
CULTIVARS: Some naturally occurring varieties that exhibit a more compact habit

Taxodium distichum - Bald Cypress

Bald Cypress is incredibly versatile, majestic, and handsome. It is tolerant of flooding, drought, and various soil types and textures. This tree can be used as a specimen or a street tree and in groupings around lakes or ponds. It is also valuable for wetland mitigation, naturalizing, and habitat enhancement. It will tolerate wet or dry areas and is one of the few conifers that shed all of its foliage during the winter.

PLANT TYPE: Deciduous, coniferous, large tree
MATURE SIZE: 50-80' in height and 25-30' in width
LEAVES: Alternate, simple, needle like and feathery; light green leaves turn reddish brown in fall
BARK: Brown or gray with long fibrous ridges that peel off in strips
FLOWERS: Monoecious, male pollen cones tan in drooping 4" long panicles; female cones are subglobose and greenish purple in color
FRUIT: Globular and about 1" across; purplish gray in color; seeds are triangular
HARDINESS: Zones 5-10, due to the large range in hardiness, it is best to select a local ecotype
FORM/SHAPE: Upright and pyramidal sometimes becoming irregular and flat-topped with age
GROWTH RATE: Moderate to fast
SOIL: I have found these trees to be adaptable to many soil conditions, but they prefer a moist, well-drained, slightly acidic, sandy loam. In the wild they usually occur in swamps, however this tree will tolerate wet or dry conditions.
LIGHT REQUIREMENTS: Full sun
DISEASE PROBLEMS: Leaf blight, twig blight, and small cankers
INSECT PROBLEMS: Bagworm, cypress moth, southern cypress beetle, and spider mites
LANDSCAPE VALUE: Specimen tree, street tree, groupings around lakes or ponds, wetland mitigation/remediation, naturalizing, and habitat enhancement. Good for wet or dry areas.
PRUNING TIME: Remove dead wood anytime
CULTIVARS: 'Autumn Gold' – golden yellow fall foliage; 'Pendens' – limb tips are pendulous

SHRUBS

Aesculus pavia - Red Buckeye

    This large native shrub is ideal for accent plantings, borders, and woodland gardens. Red Buckeye is relatively free of insect and disease problems, it is moderately drought tolerant, and it is attractive to hummingbirds and butterflies. The large red flowers stand out in any landscape. All parts of this plant are toxic to humans and livestock.

PLANT TYPE: Deciduous, broadleaf, large shrub
MATURE SIZE: 12-20' in height and width
LEAVES: Opposite, palmately compound 5(7) leaflets; dark green leaves turn to dull yellow in fall
STEM/BARK: Brown gray to light gray
FLOWERS: 4-8" long panicles of 1 ½" bright red (occasionally yellow) flowers that bloom April-May; stamens are longer than the petals
FRUIT: Subglobose, dehiscent capsule, 1 ½ -2" in diameter; capsules usually contain 2 brown seeds that are poisonous
HARDINESS: Zones 5-9, due to the large range in hardiness, it is best to select a local ecotype
FORM/SHAPE: Round top shrub (or small tree) with crooked branches
GROWTH RATE: Fast
SOIL: Adaptable to various soils, but prefers a moist, well-drained, loamy soil with a slightly acidic to neutral pH
LIGHT REQUIREMENTS: Sun or shade; flowers best in full sun
DISEASE PROBLEMS: None serious
INSECT PROBLEMS: Mites
LANDSCAPE VALUE: Accent plantings, borders, woodland gardens, butterfly gardens and naturalizing
PRUNING TIME: Late winter
CULTIVARS: 'Alba' – white flowers

Aesculus sylvatica - Painted Buckeye

Although the flowers of the Painted Buckeye are not as showy as those of the Red Buckeye, it still has its place in the landscape as a specimen or in woodland gardens. It is excellent for naturalizing and blending traditional landscapes with surrounding natural areas. The flower color may be yellowish, creamy pink, or pink. The flowers are attractive to hummingbirds and butterflies. All parts of this plant are toxic to humans and livestock.

PLANT TYPE: Deciduous, broadleaf, large shrub
MATURE SIZE: 6-20' in height and width (occasionally much larger)
LEAVES: Opposite, palmately compound 5 leaflets; dark green leaves (reddish purple as they emerge) turn to dull yellow in fall
STEM/BARK: Brown gray to light gray
FLOWERS: Borne on oblong panicles April-May; flowers are creamy pink, yellow-green, or pink; stamens are shorter than the petals
FRUIT: Capsule with 1-3 dark brown seeds
HARDINESS: Zones 6-9
FORM/SHAPE: Loose, sprawling shrub
GROWTH RATE: Moderate
SOIL: Moist, humus, slightly acidic
LIGHT REQUIREMENTS: Part shade
DISEASE PROBLEMS: None serious
INSECT PROBLEMS: None serious; Japanese beetles during flowering
LANDSCAPE VALUE: Specimen, woodland gardens, naturalizing
PRUNING TIME: Minimal needed in late winter
CULTIVARS: None common

Aronia arbutifolia - Red Chokeberry

This plant is tough and versatile with excellent wildlife value. Chokeberries are low maintenance native plants that are great for borders, groupings, buffers, habitat enhancement, mitigation, naturalizing, restoration, and stabilization. A close relative is the Black Chokeberry (*A. melanocarpa*), which occurs in the Mountains, lacks pubescence, and has a blackish colored fruit. *Aronia* is sometimes grouped in the genus *Sorbus*. Chokeberry is consumed by several species of birds.

PLANT TYPE: Deciduous, broadleaf, medium shrub
MATURE SIZE: 6-10' in height and 3-5' in width; suckering may result in much wider plants
LEAVES: Alternate, simple elliptic to elliptic-lanceolate, toothed margins, upper surface dark green, lower surface pubescent; leaves turn yellow, orange, or red in fall
STEM/BARK: Brownish and hairy (tomentose)
FLOWERS: White and borne on 9-20 flowered corymbs; bloom April-May
FRUIT: Red pome
HARDINESS: Zones 4-9, due to the large range in hardiness, it is best to select a local ecotype
FORM/SHAPE: Upright, multi-stemmed shrub; often suckering to form colonies
GROWTH RATE: Moderate
SOIL: Tolerant to many soil types; will tolerate wet or dry conditions
LIGHT REQUIREMENTS: Full sun to part shade; full sun produces best flower/fruit
DISEASE PROBLEMS: Leaf spots, blight
INSECT PROBLEMS: None serious
LANDSCAPE VALUE: Borders, groupings, buffers, habitat enhancement, mitigation, naturalizing, restoration, stabilization
PRUNING TIME: Late winter (best if left alone and excessive pruning may result in reduced flowering)
CULTIVARS: 'Brilliantissima' – more compact than species and showy red fall color

Asimina triloba - PawPaw

PawPaw is large shrub that produces a unique brownish purple flower and nice edible berries. Paw-paw fruit is a valuable food source to many species of birds and wildlife.   This multi-stemmed shrub is relatively free of disease and insect problems, and it is great for woodland gardens, naturalizing, buffers, stream-banks, and habitat enhancement.

PLANT TYPE: Deciduous, broadleaf, large shrub
MATURE SIZE: 15-20' in height and width; sometimes suckering forms large continual colonies
LEAVES: Alternate, simple, obovate, medium green leaves turn yellow in fall
STEM/BARK: Brown
FLOWERS: Brownish purple, solitary, 6 petals (3 large and 3 small)
FRUIT: Ovoid, pale green berry, turns brownish, edible
HARDINESS: Zones 6-8
FORM/SHAPE: Multi-stemmed shrub with spreading branches; can be pruned and trained to form a small pyramidal tree
GROWTH RATE: Moderate
SOIL: Moist, deep, fertile, slightly acidic
LIGHT REQUIREMENTS: Sun to light shade
DISEASE PROBLEMS: Usually none serious, but fungal leaf diseases are possible
INSECT PROBLEMS: None serious
LANDSCAPE VALUE: Woodland gardens, naturalizing, buffers, stream-banks, and habitat enhancement
PRUNING TIME: Late winter
CULTIVARS: N/A

Callicarpa americana - American Beautyberry

This is another shrub that is relatively free of disease and insect problems, and it produces a beautiful light purple fruit display that is excellent for cut stem decoration. The shrub is ideal for massing, woodland gardens, naturalizing, and habitat enhancement. Beautyberry fruit is a valuable food source for deer and many species of songbirds.

PLANT TYPE: Deciduous, broadleaf, medium shrub
MATURE SIZE: 3-8' in height and 5-7' or more in width
LEAVES: Opposite, simple, ovate, medium green, pubescent above, woolly (tomentose) beneath; turn dull yellow in fall
STEM/BARK: Light gray
FLOWERS: Lavender-pink borne in axillary cymes June-August
FRUIT: Drupe, violet
HARDINESS: Zones 5-9, due to the large range in hardiness, it is best to select a local ecotype
FORM/SHAPE: Loose, open
GROWTH RATE: Moderate
SOIL: Tolerant to most soil textures, needs ample moisture
LIGHT REQUIREMENTS: Full sun to part shade; flowering and fruiting is best in full sun
DISEASE PROBLEMS: None serious
INSECT PROBLEMS: None serious
LANDSCAPE VALUE: Massing, woodland gardens, naturalizing, and habitat enhancement
PRUNING TIME: Early spring (remove dead wood anytime)
CULTIVARS: 'Lactea' – white flowers and fruit

Calycanthus floridus - Sweet Shrub

Sweet Shrub's unique and attractive flowers make this a must have in woodland or native gardens. Both the flowers and the leaves possess a pleasant aroma. Although it prefers moisture, it is tolerant to many soil conditions and various ranges of light exposure. This plant is relatively free of insect and disease problems, and is ideal for shrub borders, woodland gardens, and naturalizing. Sweet shrub is an excellent source of deer browse.

PLANT TYPE: Deciduous, broadleaf, medium shrub
MATURE SIZE: 4-8' in height and 6-10' in width
LEAVES: Opposite, simple, ovate, aromatic, dark green
STEM/BARK: Gray-brown
FLOWERS: Solitary, maroon, fragrant, borne from leaf axils; sepals and petals similar and numerous; bloom in May
FRUIT: Brownish gray, indehiscent, capsule-like, receptacle containing ½" long achenes (seeds)
HARDINESS: Zones 5-9, due to the large range in hardiness, it is best to select a local ecotype
FORM/SHAPE: Bushy and spreading, rounded
GROWTH RATE: Moderate
SOIL: Tolerant to many soil conditions, prefers moisture
LIGHT REQUIREMENTS: Sun or shade; shrubs in sun grow more compact and dense
DISEASE PROBLEMS: None
INSECT PROBLEMS: None
LANDSCAPE VALUE: Shrub borders, woodland gardens, and naturalizing
PRUNING TIME: After flowering
CULTIVARS: 'Athens' – yellow, highly fragrant flowers, not common

Ceanothus americanus - New Jersey Tea

This is an extremely tough plant that is quite tolerant to drought conditions. Also, the fact that it can fix its own nitrogen makes it ideal for areas that have poor soil quality. Because it only grows 3 or 4 feet tall, it is a good plant for small places in the landscape. It is also ideal for native gardens, naturalizing, and difficult areas that may be dry or infertile. It produces beautiful white panicles of flowers in the summer, and the seeds provide food for turkey, bobwhite, and songbirds.

PLANT TYPE: Deciduous, broadleaf, small shrub
MATURE SIZE: 3-4' in height and 3-5' in width
LEAVES: Alternate, simple, ovate to obovate, irregularly toothed (serrulate), medium to dark green leaves
STEM/BARK: Dull green on new stems; greenish brown on older stems
FLOWERS: White, borne on terminal, corymbose-panicles June-July
FRUIT: Triangular capsule like drupe
HARDINESS: Zones 4-8, due to the large range in hardiness, it is best to select a local ecotype
FORM/SHAPE: Low growing, broad, compact shrub
GROWTH RATE: Slow
SOIL: Tolerant to soil types, but must have well-drained situation
LIGHT REQUIREMENTS: Full sun or part shade
DISEASE PROBLEMS: Fungal leaf spots, powdery mildew
INSECT PROBLEMS: Usually none serious, but lace bugs and scale are possible
LANDSCAPE VALUE: Good plant for small places in the landscape, native gardens, naturalizing, and difficult areas that may be dry or infertile
PRUNING TIME: After flowering
CULTIVARS: N/A

Cephalanthus occidentalis - Button Bush

This unique plant is a true wetland shrub that is ideal for butterfly gardens, bog gardens, wet places in the landscape, habitat enhancement, shoreline stabilization, and wetland mitigation. Button Bush produces a globular collection of creamy white flowers that attract butterflies. The seeds from this shrub provide a valuable food source for several species of waterfowl and songbirds. Button Bush is one of the most flood tolerant shrubs in the eastern U. S.

PLANT TYPE: Deciduous, broadleaf, medium shrub
MATURE SIZE: 3-6' in height and 3-4' in width
LEAVES: Opposite or sometimes whorled, simple, ovate to elliptic, dark green with red veins, turn to yellow in fall
STEM/BARK: Light gray with conspicuous lenticels
FLOWERS: Globular heads of numerous creamy white and fragrant flowers; bloom June-August
FRUIT: Nutlets
HARDINESS: Zones 5-11, due to the large range in hardiness, it is best to select a local ecotype
FORM/SHAPE: Loose open shrub
GROWTH RATE: Moderate
SOIL: Tolerant of various soil textures, but prefers moist alluvial soil. Needs moist to wet conditions for best results; is tolerant of flooding
LIGHT REQUIREMENTS: Full sun
DISEASE PROBLEMS: None serious
INSECT PROBLEMS: Mites that cause a pinkish colored gall on the leaves
LANDSCAPE VALUE: Butterfly gardens, bog gardens, wet places in the landscape, habitat enhancement, shoreline restoration/stabilization, and wetland mitigation/remediation
PRUNING TIME: Early spring
CULTIVARS: N/A

Clethra alnifolia - Summersweet Clethra, Sweet Pepper Bush

Clethra flowers produce a strong yet pleasant fragrance. This plant is used in the landscape as a specimen, shrub border, or accent plant, and is great for wet areas or shorelines. When grown in the sun they require more moisture, but produce the best flowering with more light. There are several cultivars that offer an array of growth habits and flower colors of white or pink. The fragrant flowers attract pollinators such as bees.

PLANT TYPE: Deciduous, broadleaf, medium shrub
MATURE SIZE: 4-8' in height and 4-6' in width
LEAVES: Alternate, simple, obovate to oblong, serrate, medium to dark green leaves turn yellow or golden brown in fall
STEM/BARK: Brown
FLOWERS: Racemes or panicles consisting of perfect, white (pink), highly fragrant, bell shaped flowers; bloom June-August
FRUIT: Dehiscent capsule containing many small seeds that resemble pepper, thus the other common name of Sweet Pepperbush
HARDINESS: Zones 5-9, due to the large range in hardiness, it is best to select a local ecotype
FORM/SHAPE: Upright rounded shrub, often suckering
GROWTH RATE: Slow to moderate
SOIL: Moist, slightly acidic soil; tolerates wet sites; tolerates clay soil, but prefers alluvial soil
LIGHT REQUIREMENTS: Full sun to partial shade
DISEASE PROBLEMS: None
INSECT PROBLEMS: None serious, occasionally mites
LANDSCAPE VALUE: Specimen, accenting, wet areas, shrub borders, shoreline/stream-bank restoration, and wetland mitigation/remediation
PRUNING TIME: Spring
CULTIVARS: 'Fern Valley Pink' – light green leaves, pink flowers, yellow fall leaf color; 'Hummingbird' – compact form, dark leaves, white flowers, yellow fall color; 'Sixteen Candles' – compact form with creamy white flowers

Cornus amomum - Silky Dogwood

This is a large usually multi stemmed shrub that is good for a wet area in the landscape, woodland gardens, habitat enhancement, shoreline stabilization, and wetland mitigation. Although it prefers shade, it will tolerate sun. The bright blue fruits make this shrub attractive, and they provide an excellent food source for birds and mammals. In addition to the nice fruits, the fall leaf color is a spectacular reddish purple color.

PLANT TYPE: Deciduous, broadleaf, medium shrub (or small tree)
MATURE SIZE: 6-10' in height and width
LEAVES: Opposite, simple, elliptic or ovate elliptic, dark green, turn red or purplish in fall
STEM/BARK: Reddish colored shoots; older bark is gray
FLOWERS: White, borne on open, flat cymes; bloom May-June
FRUIT: Bluish drupes
HARDINESS: Zones 4-8, due to the large range in hardiness, it is best to select a local ecotype
FORM/SHAPE: Multi-stemmed, rounded shrub becomes somewhat open with age
GROWTH RATE: Moderate to fast
SOIL: Tolerant to many soil types, but prefers an alluvial, moist soil
LIGHT REQUIREMENTS: Sun or shade (prefers shade)
DISEASE PROBLEMS: None serious (possibly powdery mildew)
INSECT PROBLEMS: Scale
LANDSCAPE VALUE: Good for a wet area in the landscape, woodland gardens, habitat enhancement, shoreline restoration/stabilization, and wetland mitigation/remediation
PRUNING TIME: Early spring
CULTIVARS: N/A

Euonymus americanus - Hearts-a-Bursting, Strawberry Bush

Hearts-a-bursting offers one of the most impressive fruit displays of any plant in this book. It is good for woodland gardens, but should be planted sparingly due to the fact that it is highly susceptible to scale.

PLANT TYPE: Deciduous, broadleaf, medium shrub
MATURE SIZE: 4-6' in height and 3-4' in width
LEAVES: Opposite, simple, lanceolate to ovate, medium green turning yellow (sometimes red) in fall
STEM/BARK: Green
FLOWERS: Light green, solitary, single or in threes, 5 petals, 5 stamens; bloom May-June
FRUIT: Warty, red capsule bears orange-red berries; become showy September-October
HARDINESS: Zones 5-9, due to the large range in hardiness, it is best to select a local ecotype
FORM/SHAPE: Loose, erect shrub, sometimes suckering
GROWTH RATE: Slow to moderate
SOIL: Tolerant, prefers moisture, but will tolerate drought
LIGHT REQUIREMENTS: Shade to part sun
DISEASE PROBLEMS: None serious
INSECT PROBLEMS: Very susceptible to Euonymus scale
LANDSCAPE VALUE: Naturalizing, woodland gardens
PRUNING TIME: Late winter to early spring
CULTIVARS: N/A

Fothergilla major — Fothergilla

This plant offers a great deal of reward in that it provides wonderful flowers in early spring and excellent leaf color in the fall, and it has minimal care requirements. A close relative is *F. gardenii*, which is generally shorter and more compact than *F. major*. *F. gardenii* has a smaller, narrower leaf with pubescence on both surfaces. When I observe plants sold as *F. gardenii*, I sometimes notice that they look more like *F. major*. After further literature review and discussions with respected nurserymen, I feel that there is some confusion within this genus. However, either species is a gem of a native landscape and restoration plant.

PLANT TYPE: Deciduous, broadleaf, medium shrub
MATURE SIZE: 4-8' (10') in height and width
LEAVES: Alternate, simple, oval to obovate, toothed; dark green turn to intense yellow sometimes orange or red in fall
STEM/BARK: Younger stems greenish, mature stems light brownish gray
FLOWERS: White terminal spikes of flowers that lack petals; stamens are numerous with white filaments and yellow anthers; bloom in March
FRUIT: Dehiscent capsule with 2 black seeds
HARDINESS: Zones 4-8, due to the large range in hardiness, it is best to select a local ecotype
FORM/SHAPE: Rounded, dense, multi stemmed, sometimes suckering shrub
GROWTH RATE: Slow to moderate
SOIL: Tolerant to clay but prefers a loamy soil; prefers slightly acidic, moist soil
LIGHT REQUIREMENTS: Partial shade to full sun
DISEASE PROBLEMS: None serious
INSECT PROBLEMS: None serious
LANDSCAPE VALUE: Specimen plantings, foundation plantings, massing, woodland gardens, buffers, and naturalizing
PRUNING TIME: After flowering
CULTIVARS: 'Mount Airy' – upright habit, yellow-orange fall color, heavy flowering selection

Hydrangea arborescens - Smooth Hydrangea

Smooth Hydrangea is an interesting plant with attractive flowers, and it is an excellent choice for woodland or shade gardens. If provided with ample shade and moisture, Smooth Hydrangeas will produce an abundance of white flowers during the summer months. The seeds are a food source for deer, turkey, and songbirds.

Cultivated Selection   **Wild Individual found in Longcreek, SC**

PLANT TYPE: Deciduous, broadleaf, medium shrub
MATURE SIZE: 3-5' in height and width
LEAVES: Opposite, simple, broadly ovate, serrate, dark green
STEM/BARK: Tan – brown, exfoliating
FLOWERS: Dull white, domed or flattened corymbs; bloom June-September
FRUIT: Dehiscent capsule containing brown dust like seeds
HARDINESS: Zones 4-9, due to the large range in hardiness, it is best to select a local ecotype
FORM/SHAPE: Broad and rounded
GROWTH RATE: Fast
SOIL: Very adaptable, prefers moist, well-drained soil
LIGHT REQUIREMENTS: Partial shade to full shade
DISEASE PROBLEMS: Bacterial wilt, powdery mildew
INSECT PROBLEMS: Aphids
LANDSCAPE VALUE: Massing, woodland gardens
PRUNING TIME: Late winter to early spring
CULTIVARS: 'Annabelle' – large inflorescence (corymb)

Hydrangea quercifolia - Oak Leaf Hydrangea

This is an excellent plant with a showy panicle of flowers and unique foliage. Oak Leaf Hydrangea is a low maintenance shrub ideal for borders, massing, naturalizing, and enhancement to the wooded under story. Its seeds are a food source for deer, turkey, and songbirds.

PLANT TYPE: Deciduous, broadleaf, medium shrub
MATURE SIZE: 4-6' in height and 6-8' in width
LEAVES: Opposite, simple, ovate, 5-7 lobed, medium green turning bronze-purple in fall
STEM/BARK: Orange-brown bark, exfoliating
FLOWERS: White, become pink tinged with age, 6-12" conical panicles, bloom May-July
FRUIT: Capsule
HARDINESS: Zones 5-9, due to the large range in hardiness, it is best to select a local ecotype
FORM/SHAPE: Upright, mound forming
GROWTH RATE: Moderate
SOIL: Moist, fertile, well drained
LIGHT REQUIREMENTS: Sun or partial shade (does best in southern states with some shade)
DISEASE PROBLEMS: None serious
INSECT PROBLEMS: None serious
LANDSCAPE VALUE: Shrub border, massing, naturalizing, enhancing under-story
PRUNING TIME: After flowering
CULTIVARS: 'Cloud Nine' – large white flowers; 'Snowflake' – large, long lasting, double white flowers; 'Snow Queen' – compact grower with large, dense white flowers

Hypericum frondosum - Golden St. Johnswort

This shrub offers a long and intense display of bright yellow flowers. Sometimes individuals of Hypericum will flower so heavily that it is hard to see any of the green leaves. They work well as borders or in massing, and they are ideal for small spaces since they only grow to three or four feet tall.

PLANT TYPE: Deciduous, broadleaf, small shrub
MATURE SIZE: 3-4' in height and 4-5' in width
LEAVES: Opposite, simple, oblong, bluish green
STEM/BARK: Brown, exfoliating
FLOWERS: Yellow, solitary, petals form a saucer that appears to hold a dense mass of stamens that are just as showy as the petals; bloom June-July
FRUIT: Brownish capsule
HARDINESS: Zones 6-8
FORM/SHAPE: Upright, rounded
GROWTH RATE: Moderate to fast
SOIL: Tolerant, but prefers moist, well-drained, rich soil with high percentage of sand
LIGHT REQUIREMENTS: Full sun to partial shade
DISEASE PROBLEMS: Anthracnose, root rot, and wilt
INSECT PROBLEMS: Thrips and scale
LANDSCAPE VALUE: Massing, shrub borders, and native gardens
PRUNING TIME: Early spring if at all
CULTIVARS: 'Sunburst' – shorter and more compact

Hypericum densiflorum - Bushy St. Johnswort

This St. Johnswort is not as showy as the previous species, but is more tolerant to drought and poor soil. It too is a small, dense shrub that produces a nice display of yellow flowers in the early summer. It can be used for massing, shrub borders, and native gardens.

PLANT TYPE: Deciduous, broadleaf, small to medium shrub
MATURE SIZE: 4-6' in height and 3-5' in width
LEAVES: Opposite, simple, elliptic, oblong, or linear, dark green
STEM/BARK: Brown, exfoliating
FLOWERS: Yellow, solitary, ½" across, dense mass of stamens that are just as showy as the petals; bloom June-July
FRUIT: Brownish capsule
HARDINESS: Zones 4-8 due to the large range in hardiness, it is best to select a local ecotype
FORM/SHAPE: Erect, freely branched
GROWTH RATE: Slow
SOIL: Tolerant, but prefers moist, well-drained, rich soil with high percentage of sand; tolerates dry sandy soils
LIGHT REQUIREMENTS: Full sun to partial shade
DISEASE PROBLEMS: Anthracnose, root rot, and wilt
INSECT PROBLEMS: Thrips and scale
LANDSCAPE VALUE: Massing, shrub borders, and native gardens
PRUNING TIME: Early spring if at all
CULTIVARS: 'Creel's Gold Star' – compact and rounded, 1-3' in height and width

Ilex glabra - Inkberry Holly

Inkberry Holly is one of the few evergreen native shrubs, which makes it ideal for foundation plantings, hedges, and massing. It has the potential to spread by means of suckering. Although it is relatively free from insect and disease problems it can be damaged or killed by excessive moisture in the soil. The fruit is an excellent food source for turkey, bobwhite, and several species of songbirds.

PLANT TYPE: Evergreen, broadleaf, medium shrub
MATURE SIZE: 6-8' in height and 8-10' in width
LEAVES: Alternate, simple, obovate, glossy, dark green
STEM/BARK: Green
FLOWERS: Male (staminate) flowers borne 3 or more flowered pedunculate cymes; female (pistillate) flowers are solitary; flowers consist of 6-8 creamy petals; bloom May-June
FRUIT: Drupe, black, globose
HARDINESS: Zones 5-9, due to the large range in hardiness, it is best to select a local ecotype
FORM/SHAPE: Upright, rounded, shrub
GROWTH RATE: Slow
SOIL: Moist and slightly acidic
LIGHT REQUIREMENTS: Full sun to partial shade
DISEASE PROBLEMS: None serious
INSECT PROBLEMS: Red mites
LANDSCAPE VALUE: Foundation plantings, hedges, massing, and native gardens
PRUNING TIME: Early spring
CULTIVARS: 'Compacta' – more compact and rounded than the species

Ilex verticillata - Winterberry Holly

This is a great shrub for adding winter color to the landscape because it produces a bright red drupe that persists through winter and into early spring. It is also useful for restoration of natural ecosystems. Winterberry Holly is best used in the landscape as a border or massing. It proves valuable when used for restoration or ecological enhancement because it is tough, versatile, and is a valuable food source for Turkey and songbirds.

PLANT TYPE: Deciduous, broadleaf, medium shrub
MATURE SIZE: 6-12' in height and width
LEAVES: Alternate, simple, obovate or oblanceolate, toothed, bright green, usually with a long pointed tip, and slightly hairy underneath
STEM/BARK: Olive to brown becomes rough with age
FLOWERS: White with green center, borne in the axils of the stem April-May
FRUIT: Bright red drupes containing pyrenes; often persist into winter and early spring; need male and female plants for fruiting to be possible
HARDINESS: Zones 5-8
FORM/SHAPE: Dense rounded shrub; usually multi-stemmed and sometimes suckering
GROWTH RATE: Slow to moderate
SOIL: Rather tolerant but prefers moist, slightly acidic, organic soil; tolerates wet conditions
LIGHT REQUIREMENTS: Full sun to partial shade
DISEASE PROBLEMS: Leaf spot and powdery mildew
INSECT PROBLEMS: None serious
LANDSCAPE VALUE: Massing, shrub borders, naturalizing, habitat enhancement, shorelines and stream-banks
PRUNING TIME: Late winter to early spring
CULTIVARS: 'Fairfax' – compact plant that produces an abundance of red fruit: 'Jackson' - male for pollinating; 'Jim Dandy' – male for pollinating; 'Jolly Red' – produces an abundance of large red fruits; 'Red Sprite' – compact, rounded, with large bright red fruit; 'Winter Red' – large, broad, female that produces persistent, bright red fruits

Ilex vomitoria - Yaupon Holly

This is another one of the few evergreen native shrubs and it is great for foundation plantings, topiary, screening, hedges, corners of buildings or large houses, buffers, xeriscapes, and mitigation. It also serves as a nice specimen. The large selections are sold as females for the showy red fruits, and these individual grow to be at least 15 to 20 feet tall. The male that pollinates the females is a dwarf that only grows to about 4 feet, and dwarf individuals work well for grouping, massing, and foundations, especially under low windows. These plants are easy to grow, drought tolerant, and relatively free from disease and insect problems. The fruit is an excellent food source for turkey, bobwhite, and several species of songbirds.

Weeping Variety (Female)

Dwarf Variety (Male)

PLANT TYPE: Evergreen, broadleaf, large shrub   (or small tree)
MATURE SIZE: 15-30' in height and 10-20' in width
LEAVES: Alternate, simple, ovate, dark green
STEM/BARK: Smooth and gray
FLOWERS: Male plants produce numerous flowered clusters in the leaf axils, female plants produce solitary or paired flowers, greenish white and bloom in April
FRUIT: Females produce red or orange drupe in fall that persist through winter
HARDINESS: Zones 7-9
FORM/SHAPE: Upright, spreading, rounded; will sucker to form thickets
GROWTH RATE: Moderate
SOIL: Tolerates dry to extremely wet soils; prefers moist well-drained fertile, humus rich soils
LIGHT REQUIREMENTS: Full sun to part shade, best flower and fruit production in full sun
DISEASE PROBLEMS: None serious
INSECT PROBLEMS: Several different scales, aphids, leaf miners, Ambrosia beetles
LANDSCAPE VALUE: Topiary, screening, hedges, specimen, corners of buildings or large houses, buffers, xeriscapes, and possible mitigation
PRUNING TIME: Late winter to early spring
CULTIVARS: 'Katherine' – abundant orange-yellow fruit; 'Pendula' – weeping branches; 'Schillings' – compact 3-4' tall and wide, male; use to pollinate larger females

Illicium floridanum - Florida Anise-tree

This is a nice evergreen shrub that produces attractive star like maroon flowers. Other than its potential to get root rot in wet or heavy soils, it is an excellent, relatively trouble free native for planting in the shade and part shade. It is used for shrub borders, large walls or corners, native gardens, naturalizing, and shady shorelines.

PLANT TYPE: Evergreen, broadleaf, medium shrub
MATURE SIZE: 6-10' in height and 4-8' in width
LEAVES: Alternate, simple, narrowly oval to lanceolate, glossy dark green, highly aromatic
STEM/BARK: Rounded, gray-brown with lenticles
FLOWERS: Nodding, star-shaped, maroon-purple, solitary flowers with many strap shape petals; bloom Late March-April
FRUIT: Dehiscent follicles; seeds are round, brown, and shiny
HARDINESS: Zones 7-9
FORM/SHAPE: Bushy, upright shrub
GROWTH RATE: Moderate
SOIL: Moist, well-drained, organic soil
LIGHT REQUIREMENTS: Tolerant, prefers full shade
DISEASE PROBLEMS: Anthracnose, crown rot, and root rot
INSECT PROBLEMS: None serious
LANDSCAPE VALUE: Shrub borders, large walls or corners, native gardens, naturalizing, and shady shorelines
PRUNING TIME: Late spring (after flowering)
CULTIVARS: 'Halley's Comet' – heavy flower production, deep red petals

Illicium parviflorum - Yellow Anise-tree

This is another evergreen Anise, however it does not offer the showy flowers that Florida Anise does. It does tolerate more sun than the Florida Anise and grows slightly larger. It's best used for massing, screening, and wetland mitigation.

PLANT TYPE: Evergreen, broadleaf, medium shrub
MATURE SIZE: 6-15' in height and 6-10' in width
LEAVES: Alternate, simple, oval, entire, green, olive green, or yellowish green depending on soil fertility, light exposure, and plant variety
STEM/BARK: Green
FLOWERS: Yellow-green, small, found in leaf axils, 6-15 petals; rather inconspicuous; appear May-June
FRUIT: Star-shaped capsule
HARDINESS: Zones 6-9
FORM/SHAPE: Upright, sometimes suckering
GROWTH RATE: Moderate
SOIL: Moist, well-drained, acidic, humus rich
LIGHT REQUIREMENTS: Sun to part shade
DISEASE PROBLEMS: Root and stem rots
INSECT PROBLEMS: None serious
LANDSCAPE VALUE: Massing, screening, wetland plantings
PRUNING TIME: Late winter
CULTIVARS: 'Forest Green' – has darker green leaves than the species

Itea virginica - Virginia Willow

Itea is a great choice for almost any situation. It is ideal for massing, woodland gardens, or planting wet places in the landscape, and this is a beautiful yet tough plant for restoration of stream banks and lake shorelines. It offers a dangling tassel like inflorescence of white flowers in the spring and a nice burgundy leaf color in the fall. The flowers are slightly fragrant and attractive to butterflies.

PLANT TYPE: Deciduous, broadleaf, small shrub
MATURE SIZE: 3-6' in height and 4-8' wide, usually due to suckering
LEAVES: Alternate, simple, elliptic or obovate, serrate or serrulate; medium green leaves turn reddish-purple in fall
STEM/BARK: Reddish
FLOWERS: White, arranged on a narrow terminal raceme, mildly fragrant; 5 sepals and petals; bloom April-May
FRUIT: Pubescent capsule containing many small seeds
HARDINESS: Zones 5-9, due to the large range in hardiness, it is best to select a local ecotype
FORM/SHAPE: Due to a great deal of variation *I. virginica* may have an upright, rounded, or arching habit
GROWTH RATE: Moderate to fast
SOIL: Tolerant to many soil types and textures, also, tolerant to a variety of pH and moisture levels; prefers moist, fertile, depositional soils; will tolerate wet soils as well as dry soils
LIGHT REQUIREMENTS: Sun or shade
DISEASE PROBLEMS: None serious
INSECT PROBLEMS: None serious
LANDSCAPE VALUE: Moist to wet areas in the landscape, massing, woodland gardens, buffers, naturalizing, shoreline restoration/stabilization, and wetland mitigation/remediation
PRUNING TIME: Early June after flowering occurs
CULTIVARS: 'Henry's Garnet' – a handsome selection that displays brilliant red-purple fall leaf color; flowers heavily and grows to 3-5'; 'Little Henry' – compact form 3-4' tall and dense; excellent red-purple fall leaf color

Kalmia latifolia - Mountain Laurel

This is a wonderful shrub, and it is one of the most beautiful flower displays of any plant I know. However, cultivation of Mountain Laurel can be difficult especially in heavy soils, and it can be quite finicky. If you are lucky enough to have natural occurrences of this plant, I suggest that you preserve it and/or incorporate it into the landscape planting design.

PLANT TYPE: Evergreen, broadleaf, medium shrub (or small tree)
MATURE SIZE: 8-12' in height and width (can grow larger)
LEAVES: Alternate, simple, elliptic to elliptic-lanceolate, thick, leathery, and dark green
STEM/BARK: Younger stems green or even reddish sometimes; older stems are brown
FLOWERS: Pink, cup-like, borne on terminal corymbs; bloom April-June
FRUIT: Brown, erect, dehiscent capsule containing tiny seeds
HARDINESS: Zones 4-9, due to the large range in hardiness, it is best to select a local ecotype
FORM/SHAPE: Dense, bushy shrub; becomes more open and loose with age
GROWTH RATE: Slow
SOIL: Acidic, humus rich, moist, well-drained; heavy soil can result in rot
LIGHT REQUIREMENTS: Deep shade to full sun (flowers best with more light)
DISEASE PROBLEMS: Leaf spot, flower blight, root rot in heavy soils
INSECT PROBLEMS: Scale, lace bug, and several borer species
LANDSCAPE VALUE: Shady borders, specimen, massing, woodland gardens, and naturalizing
PRUNING TIME: After flowering occurs
CULTIVARS: 'Alba' – pure white flowers; 'Clementine Churchill' – rich pink flowers; 'Elf' – compact, dwarf form with white flowers; 'Fuscata' – has a brownish, maroon, or cinnamon band inside the white flowers; 'Myrtifolia' – dense, compact form with small leaves and pale pink flowers; 'Pink Charm' – rich pink flowers with a red ring inside

Leucothoe axillaris - Coastal Dog-hobble

Dog hobble is beautiful especially growing along the creek banks under a dense canopy of trees. It can be temperamental in the landscape, but I have seen many cases where it is growing well and prospering over time. Wild individuals seem to perform better than cultivated ones. It can be used for foundation plantings, hillsides, massing, shrub borders and stream-banks. Dog-hobble does best in deep shade with high moisture; it is not tolerant of drought or high winds.

PLANT TYPE: Evergreen, broadleaf, medium shrub
MATURE SIZE: 4-6' in height and 5-6' in width
LEAVES: Alternate, simple, ovate, lustrous, dark green
STEM/BARK: Greenish, sometimes reddish on new growth
FLOWERS: White, urn shaped, borne on axillary racemes April-May
FRUIT: Dehiscent capsule
HARDINESS: Zones 6-9
FORM/SHAPE: Dense, spreading, somewhat weeping shrub with arching stems
GROWTH RATE: Slow to moderate
SOIL: Moist, well-drained, acidic soil
LIGHT REQUIREMENTS: Full shade to partial sun
DISEASE PROBLEMS: Leaf spot and root rot
INSECT PROBLEMS: None serious
LANDSCAPE VALUE: Shady foundation plantings, shady hillsides, massing, shrub borders and stream-banks
PRUNING TIME: Late winter to early spring
CULTIVARS: 'Sarah's Choice' – low compact form to 4', new growth is bright red

Leucothoe fontanesiana - Piedmont Dog-hobble

Although many people can't tell the difference between *L. axillaris* and *L. fontanesiana*, there are minor differences in the flowers and leaves of these plants. This plant is sold less often than *L. axillaris*, but when found and planted, it seems to perform better in the piedmont and foothills than *L. axillaris*.

PLANT TYPE: Evergreen, broadleaf, medium shrub
MATURE SIZE: 3-6' in height and 6-10' in width
LEAVES: Alternate, simple, lanceolate to ovate-lanceolate, toothed and leathery
STEM/BARK: Greenish and shiny
FLOWERS: White, urn-shaped, borne in axillary racemes; bloom April to May
FRUIT: Dehiscent capsule
HARDINESS: Zones 5-8
FORM/SHAPE: Dense, spreading, somewhat weeping shrub with arching stems
GROWTH RATE: Slow to moderate
SOIL: Moist, well-drained, acidic soil
LIGHT REQUIREMENTS: Full shade to partial sun
DISEASE PROBLEMS: Leaf spot and root rot
INSECT PROBLEMS: None serious
LANDSCAPE VALUE: Shady foundation plantings, shady hillsides, massing, shrub borders and stream-banks
PRUNING TIME: Late winter to early spring
CULTIVARS: 'Mary Elizabeth' – compact form with smaller leaves; 'Scarletta' – new growth is a dark purple color that turns to dark green with age

Lindera benzoin - Spice Bush

Spice Bush is a trouble free and easily grown shrub that is great as filler material for woodland gardens. It is also perfect for naturalizing and blending landscapes with surrounding natural areas. What it lacks in flower display, it makes up for in fall leaf color. The leaves and stems of this shrub have a pleasant aroma.

PLANT TYPE: Deciduous, broadleaf, medium shrub
MATURE SIZE: 6-10' in height and 5-8' in width
LEAVES: Alternate, simple, obovate, aromatic, green leaves turn bright yellow in fall
STEM/BARK: Green or pale greenish brown
FLOWERS: Axillary clusters of greenish yellow, star-shaped flowers; male and female flowers on different plants (dioecious) bloom March to April
FRUIT: Oval, red, drupe
HARDINESS: Zones 5-9, due to the large range in hardiness, it is best to select a local ecotype
FORM/SHAPE: Rounded shrub with upright branches
GROWTH RATE: Slow to moderate
SOIL: Tolerant, but prefers moist, well-drained soil
LIGHT REQUIREMENTS: Full sun to part shade
DISEASE PROBLEMS: None serious
INSECT PROBLEMS: None serious
LANDSCAPE VALUE: Woodland gardens, naturalizing
PRUNING TIME: Late winter to early spring
CULTIVARS: Minimal availability

Myrica cerifera - Wax Myrtle

Wax Myrtle is a large evergreen shrub that is ideal as a specimen, or it can be used for screening, large estates, commercial landscapes, xeriscapes, mitigation, buffers, and naturalizing. Some individuals tend to send up root sprouts, which can be a maintenance issue in the landscape but makes it ideal for shoreline stabilization and naturalizing. Wax Myrtle is free of insects and disease problems, and it fixes atmospheric nitrogen, which makes it tolerant to poor soils. It is also tolerant to moderate drought and salt spray. The fruit is an excellent food source for turkey, bobwhite, and many species of songbirds and waterfowl.

PLANT TYPE: Evergreen, broadleaf, large shrub
MATURE SIZE: 10-20' in height and width
LEAVES: Alternate, simple, oblanceolate, glossy green and aromatic
STEM/BARK: Gray
FLOWERS: Inconspicuous
FRUIT: Grayish, globose fruits
HARDINESS: Zones 7-9(10)
FORM/SHAPE: Rounded with upright branches
GROWTH RATE: Moderate to fast
SOIL: Tolerant, prefers moist, well-drained soils
LIGHT REQUIREMENTS: Full sun to part shade
DISEASE PROBLEMS: None serious
INSECT PROBLEMS: None serious
LANDSCAPE VALUE: Specimen, screen, large estates or commercial landscapes, xeriscapes, mitigation, buffers, and naturalizing
PRUNING TIME: Late winter to early spring
CULTIVARS: Several dwarfs that grow 2-4'

Physocarpus opulifolius – Ninebark

Ninebark is a beautiful native shrub that offers many clusters of white flowers in early spring. It is useful for borders, massing, and stream-bank or shoreline restoration. If given ample moisture and late afternoon shade it is an extremely trouble free plant. The true species has medium green leaves, but there are cultivars available that offer yellow or purplish leaf color.

PLANT TYPE: Deciduous, broadleaf, medium shrub
MATURE SIZE: 5-10' in height and width
LEAVES: Alternate, simple, ovate, 3-5 lobed, medium green
STEM/BARK: Grayish brown, exfoliating
FLOWERS: White (sometimes vaguely pinkish) borne on many flowered corymbs; each flower with 5 sepals and petals
FRUIT: Follicles containing shiny, light brown seeds
HARDINESS: Zones 3-7, due to the large range in hardiness, it is best to select a local ecotype
FORM/SHAPE: Dense shrub with arching branches
GROWTH RATE: Moderate to fast
SOIL: Extremely adaptable, but prefers moist, well-drained, fertile, slightly acidic soil
LIGHT REQUIREMENTS: Full sun to part shade
DISEASE PROBLEMS: None serious
INSECT PROBLEMS: Slugs, aphids
LANDSCAPE VALUE: Borders, massing, stream-bank and shoreline restoration/stabilization
PRUNING TIME: After flowering
CULTIVARS: 'Dart's Gold' – bright yellow new foliage, somewhat compact; 'Diablo' – reddish purple foliage

Rhododendron austrinum- Florida Azalea

This Azalea is one of the more drought tolerant Azaleas available, and it offers a wonderful display of yellow-orange flowers in spring. Florida Azalea is great for mixed shrub borders, woodland and native gardens, under story plantings and naturalizing. These shrubs work well when planted under or around Florida Dogwood, Downy Serviceberry, or Carolina Silverbell. In addition to their beauty, the flowers attract butterflies and hummingbirds.

PLANT TYPE: Deciduous, broadleaf, medium shrub
MATURE SIZE: 6-10' in height and 4-5' in width
LEAVES: Alternate, simple, elliptic to obovate, medium green, and pubescent
STEM/BARK: Young stems are a light grayish brown and older stems are dark brown
FLOWERS: Yellow to orange, occur in clusters of 8-15, slightly fragrant, tubular, bloom April-May
FRUIT: Capsule
HARDINESS: Zones 7-9
FORM/SHAPE: Upright, rounded, and often times multi-stemmed
GROWTH RATE: Moderate
SOIL: Slightly acidic, moist
LIGHT REQUIREMENTS: Part sun
DISEASE PROBLEMS: None serious; sometimes root rot
INSECT PROBLEMS: Lace bug
LANDSCAPE VALUE: Mixed shrub borders, woodland and native gardens, under story plantings, naturalizing
PRUNING TIME: After flowering occurs
CULTIVARS: 'Adam's Orange' – bright orange flowers; 'Lisa's Gold' – golden yellow flowers, bloom in April; 'My Mary' – ball shaped clusters of light yellow flowers, compact growth

Rhododendron calendulaceum - Flame Azalea

    Flame Azalea is one of the most aesthetic and showy of all the azaleas. It produces large bright orange flowers in spring and holds the flowers for long periods. It is a great shrub for massing, woodland gardens, and naturalizing, and it can even serve as a specimen. This is a parent of many hybrid azaleas produced by the nursery industry.

PLANT TYPE: Deciduous, broadleaf, medium shrub
MATURE SIZE: 6-8' in height and 8-10' in width
LEAVES: Alternate, simple, oblong-elliptic, pubescent, medium green turning yellow in fall
STEM/BARK: Gray
FLOWERS: Yellow, orange, sometimes scarlet, and many other shades of these colors; borne on lax trusses May-June
FRUIT: Capsule
HARDINESS: Zones 5-7
FORM/SHAPE: Loose, upright
GROWTH RATE: Moderate
SOIL: Moist, slightly acidic
LIGHT REQUIREMENTS: Full sun to part shade (flowers best in sun)
DISEASE PROBLEMS: Root rot
INSECT PROBLEMS: Lace bug
LANDSCAPE VALUE: Massing, naturalizing, woodland gardens
PRUNING TIME: After flowering
CULTIVARS: 'Yellow Flame' – bright yellow flower; 'Early Red Flame' – bears reddish flowers

Rhododendron canescens - Piedmont Azalea, Pinxter Azalea

When given ample moisture and shade this is a trouble free and rewarding shrub that offers an early spring display of light pink flowers. Flowering occurs early when most plants are still dormant from winter; therefore it shows up nicely in the woods. This shrub is great for woodland and native gardens, naturalizing, restoration, mitigation, and shady stream-banks or shorelines. Piedmont Azaleas attract butterflies and hummingbirds.

PLANT TYPE: Deciduous, broadleaf, large shrub
MATURE SIZE: 10-15' in height and 4-5' in width
LEAVES: Alternate, simple, elliptic to oblanceolate, medium green, and slightly pubescent
STEM/BARK: Gray
FLOWERS: Light pink to rose, sometimes white; borne in clusters of 6-19, bloom March-April
FRUIT: Capsule
HARDINESS: Zones 5-9, due to the large range in hardiness, it is best to select a local ecotype
FORM/SHAPE: Narrow, upright, and often suckering
GROWTH RATE: Moderate
SOIL: Moist, slightly acidic
LIGHT REQUIREMENTS: Shade
DISEASE PROBLEMS: None serious
INSECT PROBLEMS: None serious, possibly lace bug
LANDSCAPE VALUE: Woodland and native gardens, naturalizing, restoration/mitigation, and shady stream-banks or shorelines
PRUNING TIME: After flowering occurs
CULTIVARS: 'Camilla's Blush' – fast growing selection with pink flowers that bloom in April

Rhododendron catawbiense - Mountain Rosebay, Catawba Rhododendron

Catawbah Rhododendrons are beautiful evergreen shrubs with extremely showy flowers, however they can be difficult to grow particularly in hot and humid conditions. Proper cultural practices are important for a successful experience with this plant. They are useful for borders, foundation beds, groupings, and native gardens.

PLANT TYPE: Evergreen, broadleaf, medium shrub
MATURE SIZE: 6-10' in height and 5-9' in width
LEAVES: Alternate, simple, elliptic to oblong, glossy, dark green (light green underneath)
STEM/BARK: Young stems are light green and turn brownish with age
FLOWERS: Purple, bell-shaped; occur in large clusters, blooms in April-June depending latitude and elevation
FRUIT: Dehiscent, reddish brown, pubescent, capsule
HARDINESS: Zones 4-8, due to the large range in hardiness, it is best to select a local ecotype
FORM/SHAPE: Rounded shrub with dense foliage
GROWTH RATE: Slow
SOIL: Moist, well-drained, organic, acidic soil; good drainage is a must
LIGHT REQUIREMENTS: Full sun to part shade; more shade in zones 7 & 8
DISEASE PROBLEMS: Crown rot, root rot, petal blight, and azalea gall
INSECT PROBLEMS: Borers, Japanese beetle, lace bug, leaf miner, mealybugs, scale, and thrips
LANDSCAPE VALUE: Borders, foundation beds, groupings, and native gardens
PRUNING TIME: After flowering occurs
CULTIVARS: There are a hundred or more cultivars; I have chosen to list a few that have some resistance to heat and/or disease. 'Caroline' – (actually *R. carolinianum*) lavender-pink flowers; resistant to root rot; 'Labar's White' – white flowers, excellent heat tolerance; 'Nova Zembla' – reddish-lavender flowers, good heat tolerance

Rhododendron flammeum - Oconee Azalea

Oconee Azalea is another extremely showy shrub that produces flower clusters that can be yellow, orange or red. When flowering, these plants are covered in blooms, and they are a nice splash of color for massing, naturalizing, woodland gardens and hillsides.

PLANT TYPE: Deciduous, broadleaf, medium shrub
MATURE SIZE: 6-8' in height and 8-10' in width
LEAVES: Alternate, simple, oblong-elliptic, pubescent, medium green turning yellow in fall
STEM/BARK: Gray
FLOWERS: Yellow, orange, or orange-red, funnel shaped, borne on trusses April-May
FRUIT: Capsule
HARDINESS: Zones 6-7
FORM/SHAPE: Upright, mounded
GROWTH RATE: Moderate
SOIL: Moist, slightly acidic
LIGHT REQUIREMENTS: Full sun to part shade (flowers best in sun)
DISEASE PROBLEMS: Root rot
INSECT PROBLEMS: Lace bug
LANDSCAPE VALUE: Massing, naturalizing, woodland gardens
PRUNING TIME: After flowering
CULTIVARS: 'Scarlet Ibis' – dark orange-reddish flowers

Rhododendron minus - Piedmont Rhododendron

This is a native shrub found growing on moist slopes and stream banks of the mountains and foothills. It can be used in the landscape for shrub borders, foundations, massing, grouping, native gardens, and natural areas. While I have seen it growing in part sun it does best when shaded. The light pink flowers brighten up the woodlands during late spring and early summer. Although some have listed them as different species or varieties, most literature considers R. *carolinianun* synonymous with R. *minus*.

PLANT TYPE: Evergreen, broadleaf, medium shrub
MATURE SIZE: 6-9' in height and width
LEAVES: Alternate, simple, elliptic, leathery, dark green above, pale green with rust-like spots beneath
STEM/BARK: Young stems purplish; older stems and trunk grayish
FLOWERS: Pink, sometimes rose or white, funnel shaped; borne on 4-12 flowered terminal trusses (raceme) April-June
FRUIT: Dehiscent capsule containing seeds that are tapered at both ends
HARDINESS: Zones 5-8, due to the large range in hardiness, it is best to select a local ecotype
FORM/SHAPE: Loose, rounded shrub
GROWTH RATE: Slow
SOIL: Moist, fertile, well-drained, slightly acidic
LIGHT REQUIREMENTS: Shade to part sun
DISEASE PROBLEMS: Crown rot, dieback, root rot, leaf gall, powdery mildew, and petal blight
INSECT PROBLEMS: Lace bug, scale, aphids, borers, weevils, and Japanese beetle
LANDSCAPE VALUE: Shrub borders, foundations, massing, groupings, native gardens, and natural areas; must protect from high winds and direct sunlight
PRUNING TIME: After flowering
CULTIVARS: There are several white varieties and cultivars.

Rhododendron viscosum - Swamp Azalea

Swamp Azalea, as the name might indicate, grows in wet or boggy areas. It is ideal for wet places in the landscape, moist woodland gardens, naturalizing, wetland mitigation, and steam bank restoration. The white or sometimes pink flowers are delightful against the dark green almost blue green foliage. The flowers attract butterflies and hummingbirds. It will not tolerate drought or crown inundation, and it prefers partial sunlight.

PLANT TYPE: Deciduous, broadleaf, medium shrub
MATURE SIZE: 3-8' in height and width
LEAVES: Alternate, simple, elliptic-obovate to oblong-obovate; dark green leaves turn red in fall
STEM/BARK: Young stems green; older stems brownish
FLOWERS: White, sometimes pink, borne in clusters of 4-12, funnel shape; bloom May-June
FRUIT: Capsule
HARDINESS: Zones 4-8, due to the large range in hardiness, it is best to select a local ecotype
FORM/SHAPE: Loose, open habit; numerous spreading branches
GROWTH RATE: Slow to moderate
SOIL: Moist, well-drained, slightly acidic
LIGHT REQUIREMENTS: Part shade
DISEASE PROBLEMS: Root rot, particularly in heavy soils
INSECT PROBLEMS: Borers, lace bug
LANDSCAPE VALUE: Boggy areas, woodland gardens, naturalizing, restoration, wetland mitigation, and streambank/shoreline stabilization
PRUNING TIME: After flowering occurs
CULTIVARS: 'Pink Mist' – pink flowered selection

Sambucus canadensis - American Elder, Elderberry

This is a large shrub that is usually found growing in wetlands and along creeks and rivers, but individuals sometimes occur in the upland environment. It produces many beautiful inflorescences of white flowers in summer that result in clusters of bright purple berry like drupes. It is great for naturalizing, wet areas, habitat enhancement, stream-banks, and shorelines. Elderberry fruit is a valuable food source for dove, turkey, bobwhite, and over 50 species of songbirds.

PLANT TYPE: Deciduous, broadleaf, large shrub
MATURE SIZE: 6-12' in height and width
LEAVES: Opposite, pinnately compound, 9-11 lanceolate-oblanceolate, serrate leaflets, light to medium green
STEM/BARK: Gray to gray-brown, covered with lenticels
FLOWERS: White, borne on flat cymes June-July
FRUIT: Purplish black, berry-like drupe containing 3-5 seeds (pyrenes)
HARDINESS: Zones 4-9, due to the large range in hardiness, it is best to select a local ecotype
FORM/SHAPE: Multi-stemmed, upright with spreading branches and stoloniferous in habit
GROWTH RATE: Fast
SOIL: Tolerant to a wide variety of soil conditions, prefers adequate moisture
LIGHT REQUIREMENTS: Full sun to part shade
DISEASE PROBLEMS: Powdery mildew, dieback, and leaf spot
INSECT PROBLEMS: Various species of borers
LANDSCAPE VALUE: Naturalizing, wet areas, habitat enhancement, stream-banks, and shorelines
PRUNING TIME: Early Spring
CULTIVARS: 'Aurea' – yellow foliage and red fruit

Styrax grandifolius - Big Leaf Snowbell

Big Leaf Snowbell is commonly found in the forest, has wonderful white flowers, and nice branch structure. It is a great plant for under-story plantings and woodland gardens. It could also be used as a specimen or for naturalizing. It is not as readily available in nurseries as other Snowbell species, but I hope that will change.

PLANT TYPE: Deciduous, broadleaf, medium shrub
MATURE SIZE: 8-12' in height and 6-8' in width
LEAVES: Alternate, simple, slightly rounded to broadly ovate, dark green
STEM/BARK: Light brown
FLOWERS: White, bell-shaped, borne on 7-20 flowered racemes April-May
FRUIT: Capsule
HARDINESS: Zones 7-9
FORM/SHAPE: Spreading and open shrub
GROWTH RATE: Slow to moderate
SOIL: Moist, well-drained, slightly acidic, humus rich soil
LIGHT REQUIREMENTS: Full sun to part shade
DISEASE PROBLEMS: None serious
INSECT PROBLEMS: None serious
LANDSCAPE VALUE: Specimen, woodland gardens, naturalizing, and stream-banks
PRUNING TIME: Late winter
CULTIVARS: N/A

Vaccinium arboreum - Farkleberry, Sparkleberry

Sparkleberry, a close relative of the blueberry, is a tough and versatile shrub. It is tolerant to many soil types, textures and moisture levels. It is free of insect and disease problems, and it is extremely drought tolerant once established. Sprakleberry is ideal for under-story plantings, dry woods, xeriscapes, habitat enhancement, and naturalizing. It offers aesthetics during all seasons with white flowers in spring, dark black berries in summer and brilliant red leaves in late fall and early winter. The fruit is a berry that can be eaten by humans, and it is a valuable food source for turkey, bobwhite, small mammals, and several species of songbirds.

PLANT TYPE: Evergreen to deciduous depending on location, broadleaf, large shrub
MATURE SIZE: 8-25' in height and width
LEAVES: Alternate, simple, oval-elliptic, dark green, leathery; brilliant orange-red in fall
STEM/BARK: Gray, brown, reddish brown; bark exfoliates
FLOWERS: White, bell-shaped, 5-lobed corolla; borne on racemes April-May
FRUIT: Green, turns to black, round persistent berries with 8-10 seeds, edible but not pleasant to eat
HARDINESS: Zones 7-9
FORM/SHAPE: Spreading shrub to small tree; pruning technique can enhance either of these forms
GROWTH RATE: Moderate
SOIL: Tolerant to many soils from sandy to heavy clay and everything in between; does best in moist, well-drained loamy soil; extremely tolerant to drought once established
LIGHT REQUIREMENTS: Sun to part shade
DISEASE PROBLEMS: None serious
INSECT PROBLEMS: None serious
LANDSCAPE VALUE: Under-story plantings, dry woods, xeriscapes, habitat enhancement, and naturalizing
PRUNING TIME: Late winter
CULTIVARS: N/A

Vaccinium ashei - Rabbiteye Blueberry, Southern Highbush Blueberry

Blueberry is a super shrub, when planted in a place with full sun and good drainage this is a trouble free plant that produces plenty of tasty fruits for humans and wildlife to enjoy. They are great for gardens, massing, naturalizing, and habitat enhancement. Rabbiteye blueberry is similar to Highbush Blueberry (*V. corymbosum*), but it is more tolerant to heat and drought. For best pollination to occur, blueberries should be planted in groups of 3-4 or more individuals with at least 2 different cultivars. All blueberry species are an excellent food source to many species of wildlife.

PLANT TYPE: Semi-evergreen to deciduous depending on location, broadleaf, medium shrub
MATURE SIZE: 6-10' in height and width
LEAVES: Alternate, simple, oblanceolate, bluish green; turn reddish orange in fall
STEM/BARK: Young stems are green to reddish and older stems are grayish; older stems are sometimes exfoliating
FLOWERS: White, urn-shaped; bloom March-May
FRUIT: Light purple, turns to dark blue, round berries; edible and quite delicious
HARDINESS: Zones 7-9
FORM/SHAPE: Upright, rounded, multi-stemmed
GROWTH RATE: Slow to moderate
SOIL: Moist, well-drained, acidic, organic
LIGHT REQUIREMENTS: Full sun to partial shade
DISEASE PROBLEMS: None serious; root rot is possible in heavy soils
INSECT PROBLEMS: None serious
LANDSCAPE VALUE: Gardens, massing, naturalizing, and habitat enhancement
PRUNING TIME: After fruiting occurs
CULTIVARS: 'Climax' – upright and open, early season fruiting, dark blue, medium size berries with good flavor; 'Premier' – vigorous upright growth, early season fruiting, quite productive; 'Tifblue' – vigorous, upright growth, mid season fruiting, large light blue berries

Vaccinium corymbosum - Highbush Blueberry

    Blueberry is a super shrub, when planted in a place with full sun and good drainage this is a trouble free plant that produces plenty of tasty fruits for humans and wildlife to enjoy. They are great for gardens, massing, naturalizing, and habitat enhancement. For best pollination to occur, blueberries should be planted in groups of 3-4 or more individuals with at least 2 different cultivars. All blueberry species are an excellent food source to many species of wildlife.

PLANT TYPE: Semi-evergreen to deciduous depending on location, broadleaf, medium shrub
MATURE SIZE: 6-12' in height and width
LEAVES: Alternate, simple, elliptic-lanceolate, bluish green; turn reddish orange in fall
STEM/BARK: Young stems are green to reddish and older stems are grayish; older stems are sometimes exfoliating
FLOWERS: White, urn-shaped; bloom in May
FRUIT: Dark blue, round berries, edible and quite delicious
HARDINESS: Zones 3-7, due to the large range in hardiness, it is best to select a local ecotype
FORM/SHAPE: Upright, rounded, multi-stemmed
GROWTH RATE: Slow
SOIL: Moist, well-drained, acidic, organic
LIGHT REQUIREMENTS: Full sun to partial shade
DISEASE PROBLEMS: None serious; root rot is possible in heavy soils
INSECT PROBLEMS: None serious
LANDSCAPE VALUE: Gardens, massing, naturalizing, and habitat enhancement
PRUNING TIME: After fruiting occurs
CULTIVARS: 'Bluecrop' – midseason fruiting, highly productive, drought tolerant; 'Earliblue' – early fruiting, vigorous growth, sweet berries; 'Jersey' – late fruiting, vigorous, with large light blue berries

Viburnum acerifolium - Mapleleaf Viburnum

This is an excellent woodland shrub that is extremely tough and trouble free. This drought tolerant plant offers a nice inflorescence of white flowers in spring followed by late summer fruits that are a valuable food source for birds and mammals. In shade or part sun, it is an easily grown shrub for massing, woodland gardens, naturalizing, and habitat enhancement.

PLANT TYPE: Deciduous, broadleaf, medium shrub
MATURE SIZE: 4-6' in height and 3-4' in width
LEAVES: Opposite, simple, 3-lobed, pubescent, dark green; turn orange, red, or purple in fall
STEM/BARK: Young stems green; older stems gray to brown
FLOWERS: White, borne on terminal cymes May-June
FRUIT: Drupe, ellipsoid, blue-black
HARDINESS: Zones 4-8, due to the large range in hardiness, it is best to select a local ecotype
FORM/SHAPE: Loose, upright shrub; tends to sucker and form colonies
GROWTH RATE: Moderate
SOIL: Tolerant, but prefers moist, well-drained loam; adapted to dry soils
LIGHT REQUIREMENTS: Shade to part shade
DISEASE PROBLEMS: None serious
INSECT PROBLEMS: None serious, possibly aphids
LANDSCAPE VALUE: Massing, native gardens, habitat enhancement, and naturalizing
PRUNING TIME: After flowering
CULTIVARS: N/A

Viburnum cassinoides - Witherod Viburnum

Like all Viburnums this shrub offers a nice display of white flowers in the spring followed by late summer and early fall fruits that are attractive and a valuable food source for wildlife. The fruits, which are drupes, offer an extended aesthetic display as they mature. The drupes first appear green; then as they mature, they turn pinkish and eventually dark blue. Witherod is relatively free of disease and insect problems, and it is ideal for shrub borders, massing, naturalizing, mitigation, habitat enhancement, shorelines, and stream-banks.

PLANT TYPE: Deciduous, broadleaf, medium shrub
MATURE SIZE: 6-10'(15') in height and 6-8' in width
LEAVES: Opposite, simple, ovate, usually dentate but sometimes nearly entire, dull green turning orange-red or purple in fall
STEM/BARK: Gray to brown
FLOWERS: Creamy white, borne on flat topped cymes June-July
FRUIT: Drupe, begins green, then turns pink and eventually turns blue-black
HARDINESS: Zones 3-8, due to the large range in hardiness, it is best to select a local ecotype
FORM/SHAPE: Dense and rounded
GROWTH RATE: Moderate
SOIL: Moist, fertile, humus rich, slightly acidic
LIGHT REQUIREMENTS: Full sun to part shade
DISEASE PROBLEMS: None serious, possibly dieback
INSECT PROBLEMS: Aphids
LANDSCAPE VALUE: Shrub borders, massing, naturalizing, mitigation, habitat enhancement, shorelines, and stream-banks
PRUNING TIME: After flowering if at all
CULTIVARS: N/A

Viburnum dentatum - Arrowwood Viburnum

Arrowwood is my pick of all the Viburnums because it is a tough, adaptable shrub. While it is best grown in part sun and moist soil with good drainage, it has the ability to adapt to sun or shade and wet or dry conditions. It can be used for grouping, massing, woodland and native gardens, buffers, naturalizing, habitat enhancement, restoration, and slope stabilization. Even with all its adaptability, it still offers a beautiful display of white flowers in spring followed by extremely showy blue fruits. The fruits, which are drupes, provide an excellent food source for birds and small mammals.

PLANT TYPE: Deciduous, broadleaf, medium shrub
MATURE SIZE: 6-10' in height and 6-12' in width
LEAVES: Opposite, simple, ovate, dark green; turn yellow, sometimes red, or purple in fall
STEM/BARK: Gray to grayish brown
FLOWERS: White or creamy white, borne on terminal cymes May-June
FRUIT: Drupe, oval, blue-black
HARDINESS: Zones 3-8, due to the large range in hardiness, it is best to select a local ecotype
FORM/SHAPE: Rounded shrub with spreading branches
GROWTH RATE: Moderate to fast
SOIL: Extremely tolerant to wide range of soil types, textures and moisture levels
LIGHT REQUIREMENTS: Sun to part shade
DISEASE PROBLEMS: Die back, leaf spots, and wood rot
INSECT PROBLEMS: Aphids, scale, Japanese beetle
LANDSCAPE VALUE: Grouping, massing, woodland and native gardens, buffers, naturalizing, habitat enhancement, restoration, and slope stabilization
PRUNING TIME: After flowering
CULTIVARS: 'Autumn Jazz' – 8-10' in height, glossy summer foliage turns yellow, orange, or burgundy in the fall; 'Blue Muffin' – Compact form, flowers and fruits heavily

Xanthorhiza simplicissima – Yellowroot

Yellowroot is a groundcover like shrub that is short and spreading. It forms large thickets and is an ideal ground cover for moist and/or shady areas, naturalizing, and shady stream banks or shorelines. If given ample moisture this is a trouble free plant that is an excellent alternative to exotic ground covers like English ivy.

PLANT TYPE: Deciduous, broadleaf, small, woody, groundcover
MATURE SIZE: 2-3' in height and indeterminate spread (suckers from roots)
LEAVES: Alternate, pinnately compound, 3-5 leaflets, pubescent, ovate, light green turn to golden yellow in fall
STEM/BARK: Yellowish gray on outside and dark yellow on inside
FLOWERS: Brownish-purple, star-shaped, borne on drooping racemose panicles April-May
FRUIT: Follicle with reddish ovoid seeds
HARDINESS: Zones 3-9, due to the large range in hardiness, it is best to select a local ecotype
FORM/SHAPE: Thicket forming, woody, ground cover with erect stems
GROWTH RATE: Moderate
SOIL: Tolerant to soil texture, prefers moist, slightly acidic soil
LIGHT REQUIREMENTS: Shade to part sun
DISEASE PROBLEMS: None serious
INSECT PROBLEMS: None serious
LANDSCAPE VALUE: Ground cover for moist and/or shady areas, naturalizing, and shady stream banks or shorelines
PRUNING TIME: After flowering if at all
CULTIVARS: N/A

Yucca filamentosa - Adam's Needle, Bear-Grass

This is a unique shrub that doesn't look like a plant that would be native to the Eastern United States, but it is. This tough plant, that is free of insect and disease problems, is extremely drought tolerant. It produces a spectacular showy stalk of white flowers. The leaves are coarse, stiff, and covered with curly thread like fibers. It is ideal for massing, rock gardens, and xeriscapes.

PLANT TYPE: Evergreen, broadleaf, small shrub
MATURE SIZE: Leaves: 1.5 –2' in height and 2-4' in width; flower stalks: 3-6' in height
LEAVES: Basal rosettes, inversely lance shaped, rigid, erect and spreading; margins fray into curly threads
STEM/BARK: Underground or nearly so
FLOWERS: White, borne on 3-6' conical panicles; bloom May-July
FRUIT: Capsule containing black, flattened seeds
HARDINESS: Zones 5-10, due to the large range in hardiness, it is best to select a local ecotype
FORM/SHAPE: Clump-forming shrub; somewhat palm-like
GROWTH RATE: Moderate to slow
SOIL: Tolerant of most soils; will not tolerate wet soils
LIGHT REQUIREMENTS: Full sun to light shade
DISEASE PROBLEMS: None serious
INSECT PROBLEMS: None serious
LANDSCAPE VALUE: Massing, rock gardens, and xeriscapes
PRUNING TIME: Remove flowering stalks in late summer
CULTIVARS: Several cultivars exist that exhibit various forms of variegation

VINES

Bignonia capreolata - Cross Vine

Cross Vine is a fast growing vine that produces an amazing display of reddish and yellow funnel shaped flowers. It is best grown on a structure rather than the ground for maintenance reasons. An instance where it might prove ideal to grow this plant on the ground is on a large bank that needs erosion control. Cross Vine attracts hummingbirds, and is a valuable food source for deer and swamp rabbits. A synonym for this plant is *Anisostichus capreolatus*.

PLANT TYPE: Evergreen to semi-evergreen, broadleaf, large vine
MATURE SIZE: 40-60' in height
LEAVES: Opposite, compound, 2 leaflets and terminal tendrils, oblong-lanceolate, dark green, lustrous; purplish during winter
STEM/BARK: Reddish, a cut stem reveals a cross shaped center (pith)
FLOWERS: Brownish red on outside and yellowish orange on inside, funnel shape, 5 lobes, April-May
FRUIT: Flattened capsule with papery, winged seeds
HARDINESS: Zones 6-9
FORM/SHAPE: Climbing vine, climbs by tendrils
GROWTH RATE: Fast
SOIL: Moist, well-drained
LIGHT REQUIREMENTS: Sun or shade, best flowering in sun
DISEASE PROBLEMS: Powdery mildew
INSECT PROBLEMS: None serious
LANDSCAPE VALUE: Fences, walls, trellis, or arbors. Has an extremely showy flower
PRUNING TIME: After flowering
CULTIVARS: 'Tangerine Beauty' – vigorous, heavily flowering selection with more of a reddish orange flower

Campis radicans - Trumpet Vine

This is another fast growing vine that offers a nice flower display, however this vine is very aggressive and sends up root sprouts that will take over the garden. Restrict the use of this plant to naturalizing or erosion control in wild or open areas. This vine does attract hummingbirds and is a valuable food source for deer.

PLANT TYPE: Deciduous, broadleaf, large vine
MATURE SIZE: 30-40' in height
LEAVES: Opposite, pinnately compound, 9-11 ovate leaflets
STEM/BARK: Light brown turning grayish with maturity; equipped with rootlets for climbing and clinging
FLOWERS: Bright orange with yellow throat, tubular, 5 lobes, June-September
FRUIT: Long narrow capsule containing 2 winged seeds
HARDINESS: Zones 4-9, due to the large range in hardiness, it is best to select a local ecotype
FORM/SHAPE: Climbing and clinging, suckers
GROWTH RATE: Very fast
SOIL: Tolerant to almost any soil situation.
LIGHT REQUIREMENTS: Full sun to part shade
DISEASE PROBLEMS: Powdery mildew
INSECT PROBLEMS: None serious
LANDSCAPE VALUE: Fences, arbors, erosion control on large banks or shorelines and stream-banks, has beautiful flowers but can be a rampant suckering vine that requires maintenance to control
PRUNING TIME: After flowering
CULTIVARS: There are a few cultivars known but they are not commonly found.

Decumaria barbara - Climbing Hydrangea, Wood Vamp

This is a great vine because it is easy to manage and is beautiful in appearance even when not in flower. Unlike most vines that want an abundance of sunlight, Wood Vamp does great in part shade. When given ample moisture this is a trouble free vine that is great for planting near a tree in woodland gardens or on an arbor, trellis, wall, or some other structure. They produce an elegant cluster of white flowers in the late spring.

PLANT TYPE: Deciduous, broadleaf, medium vine
MATURE SIZE: 20-30' in height
LEAVES: Opposite, simple, ovate-oblong, lustrous, dark green
STEM/BARK: Brown
FLOWERS: White, terminal corymbs, May-June
FRUIT: Capsule containing lustrous yellow seeds
HARDINESS: Zones 5-9, due to the large range in hardiness, it is best to select a local ecotype
FORM/SHAPE: Climbing
GROWTH RATE: Fast
SOIL: Moist, well-drained, slightly acidic, organic, loam
LIGHT REQUIREMENTS: Shade to part shade
DISEASE PROBLEMS: None serious
INSECT PROBLEMS: None serious
LANDSCAPE VALUE: Arbors, trellis, fences, and because it is not as aggressive as most vines I would even recommend it on a tree or wall.
PRUNING TIME: After flowering
CULTIVARS: 'Chattooga' – smaller leaves and more vibrant fall color than the species

Gelsemium rankinii - Swamp Jessamine

    This is an excellent multi-seasonal flowering vine that offers a spectacular show of yellow flowers in the spring and fall. It has one of the most intense flower displays of any plant that I know, and it is one of the first plants to flower in the spring. It is trouble free and easy to grow. Jessamine can be grown on a fence, mailbox, arbor, or trellis. It is also great for a large bank or slope. Jessamine is a useful source of nectar for Ruby-throated hummingbirds (despite the fact that it has yellow flowers rather than red ones) and Spicebush Swallowtail Butterfly. All parts of the plant are poisonous to humans and livestock.

PLANT TYPE: Evergreen, broadleaf, medium vine
MATURE SIZE: 20-30' in height
LEAVES: Opposite, simple, lanceolate, lustrous, dark green
STEM/BARK: Youngest stems are greenish, older shoots are reddish brown, and the most mature stems are grayish and woody with fissures
FLOWERS: Yellow, solitary, funnel-shaped, 5 sepals and 5 petal lobes, March-April and October-November
FRUIT: Capsule containing many flat and winged seeds
HARDINESS: Zones 6-9
FORM/SHAPE: Twining, climbing vine or mounding ground cover
GROWTH RATE: Moderate to fast
SOIL: Tolerant to a wide range of soils, prefers a moist, well-drained organic, fertile soil; will tolerate wet soil conditions
LIGHT REQUIREMENTS: Full sun to part shade
DISEASE PROBLEMS: None serious
INSECT PROBLEMS: None serious
LANDSCAPE VALUE: Best used on a fence, mailbox, arbor, trellis, etc, but can be used as a groundcover as well; extremely beautiful flower display
PRUNING TIME: After flowering and as needed
CULTIVARS: 'Butterscotch' – heavy flowering selection with extended display time

Gelsemium sempervirens - Carolina Jessamine, Yellow Jessamine

Yellow Jessamine is an excellent flowering vine that offers a spectacular show of yellow flowers in early spring. It has one of the most intense flower displays of any plant that I know, and it is one of the first plants to flower in the spring. It is trouble free and easy to grow. Yellow Jessamine can be grown on a fence, mailbox, arbor, or trellis. It is also great for a large bank or slope. It is sometimes referred to as Carolina Jessamine, which may be due to the fact that it is quite common in the Carolinas and is the South Carolina state flower. Jessamine is a useful source of nectar for Ruby-throated hummingbirds (despite the fact that it has yellow flowers rather than red ones) and Spicebush Swallowtail Butterfly. All parts of the plant are poisonous to humans and livestock.

PLANT TYPE: Evergreen, broadleaf, medium vine
MATURE SIZE: 20-30' in height
LEAVES: Opposite, simple, lanceolate, lustrous, dark green
STEM/BARK: Youngest stems are greenish, older shoots are reddish brown, and the most mature stems are grayish and woody with fissures
FLOWERS: Yellow, fragrant, solitary, funnel-shaped, 5 sepals and 5 petal lobes, February-March
FRUIT: Capsule containing many flat and winged seeds
HARDINESS: Zone 6-9
FORM/SHAPE: Twining, climbing vine or mounding ground cover
GROWTH RATE: Moderate to fast
SOIL: Tolerant to a wide range of soils, prefers a moist, well-drained organic, fertile soil
LIGHT REQUIREMENTS: Full sun to part shade
DISEASE PROBLEMS: None serious
INSECT PROBLEMS: None serious
LANDSCAPE VALUE: Best used on a fence, mailbox, arbor, trellis, etc, but can be used as a groundcover as well; extremely beautiful flower display
PRUNING TIME: After flowering and as needed
CULTIVARS: 'Pride of Augusta' – double flowered

Lonicera sempervirens - Coral Honey Suckle

Coral Honey Suckle is nice vine that produces many clusters of slender tube like red flowers in spring. This honey suckle is not as aggressive as Japanese Honeysuckle and it is ideal for growing on a fence, trellis, mailbox, arbor, or even up a tree in the woodland garden. The beautiful red flowers attract hummingbirds quite well.

PLANT TYPE: Deciduous, broadleaf, medium vine
MATURE SIZE: 15-20' in height
LEAVES: Opposite, simple, elliptic to obovate, 1 to 2 pairs closest to the inflorescence joined around the stem (connate)
STEM/BARK: Reddish brown
FLOWERS: Red, tubular, 5 lobes, borne on 2-4 flowered spikes April-May
FRUIT: Glossy, black, berry
HARDINESS: Zones 4-9, due to the large range in hardiness, it is best to select a local ecotype
FORM/SHAPE: Twining, climbing vine
GROWTH RATE: Fast
SOIL: Moist, well-drained
LIGHT REQUIREMENTS: Full sun to part shade
DISEASE PROBLEMS: None serious
INSECT PROBLEMS: Aphids
LANDSCAPE VALUE: Best used on a fence, mailbox, arbor, trellis, etc
PRUNING TIME: After flowering
CULTIVARS: 'Sulphurea' – yellow flowers

Native Woody Plants for Wet Sites, Stream-banks, or Shorelines

Trees:
Acer rubrum (Red Maple)
Alnus serrulata (Hazel Alder)
Betula nigra (River Birch)
Carpinus caroliniana (American Hornbeam)
Fraxinus pennsylvatica (Green Ash)
Halesia carolina (Carolina Silverbell)
Liquidambar styraciflua (Sweetgum)
Nyssa sylvatica (Black Gum)
Platanus occidentalis (Sycamore)
Quercus lyrata (Overcup Oak)
Sabal palmetto (Cabbage Palmetto)
Taxodium distichum (Bald Cypress)

Shrubs:
Cephalanthus occidentalis (Button Bush)
Clethra alinfolia (Summersweet Clethra)
Cornus amomum (Silky Dogwood)
Illicium floridanum (Florida Anise)
Itea virginica (Virginia Willow)
Leucothoe axillaries (Coastal Dog-hobble)
Leucothoe fontanesiana (Dog-hobble)
Physocarpus opulifolius (Ninebark)
Rhododendron viscosum (Swamp Azalea)
Sambucus canadensis (Elderberry)
Xanthoriza simplicissima (Yellow Root)

Vines:
Decumeria barbara (Climbing Hydrangea)

Native Woody Plants for Dry Sites

Trees:
Ilex opaca (American Holly)
Juniperus virginiana (Eastern Red Cedar)
Liquidambar styraciflua (Sweetgum)
Magnolia grandiflora (Southern Magnolia)
Quercus alba (White Oak)
Quercus coccinea (Scarlet Oak)
Quercus phellos (Willow Oak)
Quercus prinus (Chestnut Oak)
Quercus shumardii (Shumard Oak)

Shrubs:
Aronia arbutifolia (Chokeberry)
Ceanothus americanus (New Jersey Tea)
Ilex vomitoria (Yaupon Holly)
Kalmia latifolia (Mountain Laurel)
Myrica cerifera (Wax Myrtle)
Vaccinium arboreum (Sparkleberry)
Yucca filamentosa (Adam's Needle Yucca)

Native Woody Plants with Showy Flowers

Trees:
Amelanchier arborea (Serviceberry)
Cercis canadensis (Eastern Red Bud)
Chionanthus virginicus (Grancy Gray Beard)
Cornus florida (Flowering Dogwood)
Halesia carolina (Silverbell)
Hamamelis virginiana (Witch Hazel)
Liriodendron tulipifera (Tulip Poplar)
Magnolia grandiflora (Southern Magnolia)

Shrubs:
Aesculus pavia (Red Buckeye)
Aesculus sylvatica (Painted Buckeye)
Calycanthus floridus (Sweetshrub)
Ceanothus americanus (New Jersey Tea)
Cephalanthus occidentalis (Button Bush)
Clethra alnifolia (Summersweet Clethra)
Cornus amomum (Silky Dogwood)
Fothergilla major (Fothergilla)
Hydrangea arborescens (Smooth Hydrangea)
Hydrangea quercifolia (Oakleaf Hydrangea)
Hypericum frondosum (Golden St. Johnswort)
Hypericum densiflorum (Bushy St. Johnswort)
Illicium floridanum (Florida Anise)
Itea virginica (Virginia Willow)
Kalmia latifolia (Mountain Laurel)
Leucothoe axillaris (Coastal Dog-hobble)
Leucothoe fontanesiana (Dog-hobble)
Physocarpus opulifolius (Ninebark)
Rhododendron austrinum (Florida Azalea)
Rhododendron calendulaceum (Flame Azalea)
Rhododendron canescens (Piedmont Azalea)
Rhododendron catawbiense (Catawba Rhododendron)
Rhododendron flammeum (Oconee Azalea)
Rhododendron minus (Piedmont Rhododendron)
Rhododendron viscosum (Swamp Azalea)
Sambucus canadensis (Elderberry)
Styrax grandifolius (Bigleaf Snowbell)
Viburnum acerifolia (Mapleleaf Viburnum)
Viburnum cassinoides (Witherod Viburnum)
Viburnum dentatum (Arrowwood Viburnum)
Yucca filamentosa (Adam's Needle Yucca)

Vines:
Bignonia capreolata (Crossvine)
Campis radicans (Trumpet Vine)
Gelsemium rankinii (Swamp Jessamine)
Gelsemium sempervirens (Yellow Jessamine)
Lonicera sempervirens (Coral Honey Suckle)

Native Woody Plants with Showy Fruits

Trees:
Cornus florida (Flowering Dogwood)
Halesia carolina (Silverbell)
Ilex opaca (American Holly)
Magnolia grandiflora (Southern Magnolia)
Sabal palmetto (Cabbage Palmetto)

Shrubs:
Aronia arbutifolia (Red Chokeberry)
Callicarpa americana (American Beautyberry)
Cornus amomum (Silky Dogwood)
Euyonomus americanus (Hearts-A-Burstin)
Ilex verticillata (Winterberry Holly)
Ilex vomitoria (Yaupon Hollies)
Sambucus canadensis (Elderberry)
Vaccinium ashei (Rabbiteye Blueberry)
Vaccinium corymbosum (Highbush Blueberry)
Viburnum cassinoides (Witherod Viburnum)
Viburnum dentatum (Arrowwood Viburnum)

Native Woody Plants with Attractive Fall Color

Trees:
Acer rubrum (Red Maple)
Acer saccharum (Sugar Maple)
Amelanchier arborea (Serviceberry)
Cornus florida (Flowering Dogwood)
Liquidambar styraciflua (Sweetgum)
Liriodendron tulipifera (Tulip Polar)
Nyssa sylvatica (Black Gum)
Oxydendrum arboreum (Sourwood)
Quercus coccinea (Scarlet Oak)

Shrubs:
Aronia arbutifolia (Chokeberry)
Cornus amomum (Silky Dogwood)
Fothergilla major (Fothergilla)
Itea virginica (Virginia Willow)
Lindera benzoin (Spicebush)
Vaccinium arboreum (Sparkleberry)
Viburnum cassinoides (Witherod Viburnum)
Viburnum dentatum (Arrowwood Viburnum)

Native Woody Plants that are Evergreen

Trees:
Ilex opaca (American Holly)
Juniperus viginiana (Eastern Red Cedar)
Magnolia grandiflora (Southern Magnolia)
Pinus strobus (White Pine)
Quercus virginiana (Live Oak)
Sabal palmetto (Cabbage Palmetto)

Shrubs:
Ilex glabra (Inkberry Holly)
Ilex vomitoria (Yaupon Holly)
Illicium floridanum (Florida Anise)
Illicium parviflorum (Yellow Anise)
Kalmia latifolia (Mountain Laurel)
Leucothoe axillaris (Coastal Dog-hobble)
Leucothoe fontanesiana (Dog-hobble)
Myrica cerifera (Wax Myrtle)
Rhododendron catawbiense (Catawba Rhododendron)
Rhododendron minus (Piedmont Rhododendron)
Yucca filamentosa (Adam's Needle Yucca)

Vines:
Bignonia capreolata (Crossvine)
Gelsemium rankinii (Swamp Jessamine)
Gelsemium sempervirens (Yellow Jessamine)

Native Woody Plants that Provide Wildlife Food

Trees:
Acer rubrum (Red Maple)
Acer saccharum (Sugar Maple)
Alnus serrulata (Hazel Alder)
Amelanchier arborea (Serviceberry)
Carpinus caroliniana (American Hornbeam)
Chionanthus virginicus (Grancy Gray-beard)
Diospyros virginiana (Persimmon)
Fagus grandifolia (American Beech)
Hamamelis virginiana (Common Witchhazel)
Ilex opaca (American Holly)
Juniperus virginiana (Eastern Red Cedar)
Nyssa sylvatica (Black Gum)
Ostrya viginiana (American Hophornbeam)
Pinus strobus (White Pine)
Quercus alba (White Oak)
Quercus coccinea (Scarlet Oak)
Quercus lyrata (Overcup Oak)
Quercus palustris (Pin Oak)
Quercus phellos (Willow Oak)
Quercus prinus (Chestnut Oak)
Quercus shumardii (Shumard Oak)
Quercus virginiana (Live Oak)
Sabal palmetto (Cabbage Palmetto)

Shrubs:
Aronia arbutifolia (Red Chokeberry)
Asimina triloba (Paw-Paw)
Callicarpa americana (American Beautyberry)
Ceanothus americanus (New Jersey Tea)
Cephalanthus occidentalis (Button Bush)
Cornus amomum (Silky Dogwood)
Hydrangea arborescens (Smooth Hydrangea)
Hydrangea quercifolia (Oakleaf Hydrangea)
Ilex glabra (Inkberry Holly)
Ilex verticillata (Winterberry Holly)
Ilex vomitoria (Yaupon Holly)
Myrica cerifera (Wax Myrtle)
Sambucus canadensis (Elderberry)
Vaccinium arboreum (Sparkleberry)
Vaccinium ashei (Rabbiteye Blueberry)
Vaccinium corymbosum (Highbush Blueberry)
Viburnum cassinoides (Witherod Viburnum)
Viburnum dentatum (Arrowwood Viburnum)

Vines:
Bignonia capreolata (Crossvine)

USDA Hardiness Zone Map

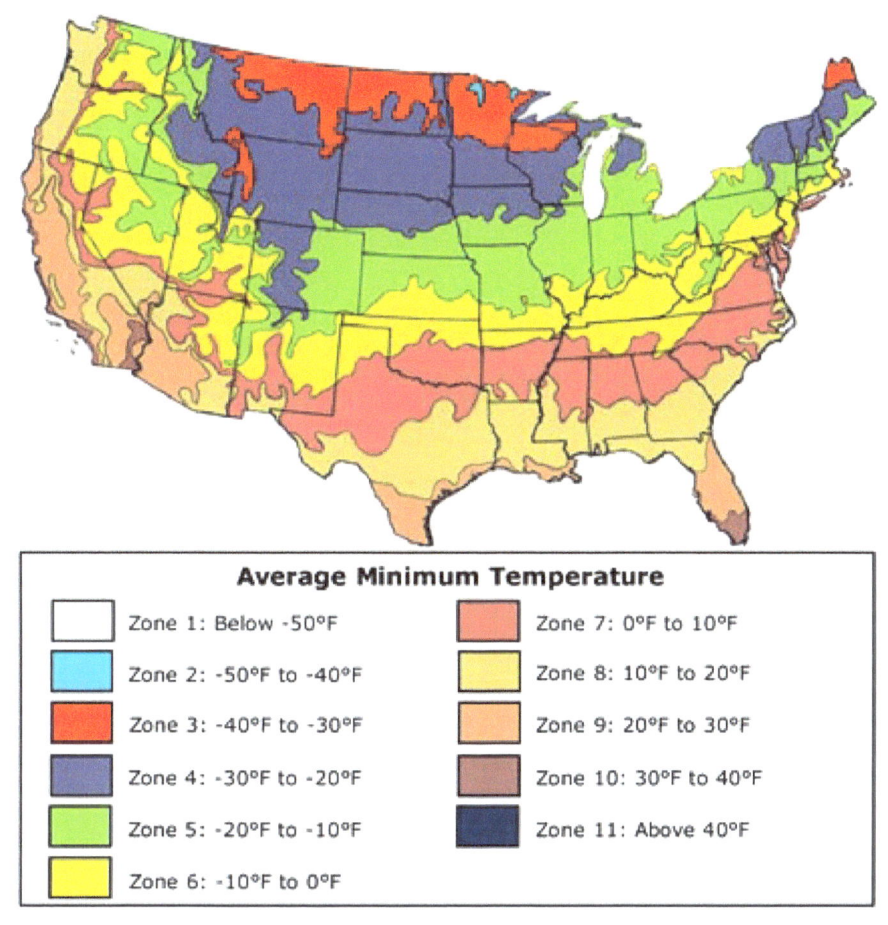

Glossary

Acorn: the fruit of the genus *Quercus* (oaks) a nut held in a woody cup-like base.
Alternate: arrangement of the leaves on the stem; the leaves are attached to the stem in a staggered formation.
Axillary: arising from the axil.
Bark: the outer protective tissue on the trunk, stem, or root of woody plants.
Berry: a fleshy, multi-seeded fruit resulting from a single ovary.
Bi-: prefix indicating two, twice, or double.
Bipinnate: twice pinnate.
Bract: a reduced leaf or leaf-like structure associated with a flower or inflorescence.
Bud: a structure of embryonic tissue that will become a stem shoot, leaf, or flower.
Capsule: a dry dehiscent (splits open to release seeds) fruit produced from a compound pistol.
Catkin: a spike-like inflorescence made up of scaly bracts, as in the genera of *Alnus, Betula, Carpinus, Quercus,* etc.
Cone: A fruit containing numerous woody, leathery, or fleshy scales containing one or more seeds and attached to a main axis.
Corymb: broad flat-topped inflorescence that opens with the outer flowers first followed by the inner flowers.
Crenate: rounded teeth on a leaf margin.
Cyme: a flat-topped inflorescence that opens with the inner flowers first followed by the outer flowers.
Cultivar: a cultivated variety
Deciduous: describes a plant that goes dormant in the winter, thus it loses its leaves in the fall.
Dehiscent: describes a fruit structure that opens or splits to release seed(s).
Dentate: having teeth along the margin that are perpendicular to that margin.
Determinate: pertaining to an inflorescence, this means that the terminal flower opens first followed by the lower flowers.
Dioecious: Male and female flowers borne on separate individuals of a species (ex: Hollies).
Dissected: divided into segments.
Drupe: a usually one seeded fruit in which the seed is surrounded by a fleshy pulp (stony endocarp).
Elliptic: broadest at the middle and narrow at the ends.
Entire: smooth leaf margins.
Evergreen: having green leaves throughout the year.
Exfoliating: peel or shed in layers, usually refers to tree bark.
Exotic: foreign, not indigenous.
Fascicle: a tight cluster usually used to describe leaves or stems.
Foliage: the leaves of a plant.
Follicle: a dry dehiscent fruit that opens along one suture.
Genus: a group of species that have similar fundamental characteristics, usually pertaining to the flower, but differ in other lesser traits.
Glabrous: not hairy, smooth.
Globose: round in shape.
Indehiscent: describes a fruit structure that does not open or split to release seed(s).
Indeterminate: pertaining to an inflorescence, this means that the terminal flower opens last.
Inflorescence: the flowering section of a plant; the arrangement of flowers on an axis.
Leaf: the primary photosynthetic structure a plant.
Lanceolate: narrow at the tip.
Legume: a dry dehiscent fruit that opens along both sutures.
Lenticel: a small spot on the plant stem made up of loosely formed cells; that allow gas exchange between plant and the atmosphere.
Linear: long and narrow when referring to a leaf.
Lobe: projecting section of the leaf or other plant organs.

Margin: edge of the leaf.
Monocot: has only one primary seed leaf as in grasses, sedges, lilies, palms, etc.
Native: original to an area, indigenous.
Nut: a dry, indehiscent, single seeded fruit that is usually hard and non fleshy.
Nutlet: a small nut-like seed that is attached to a modified leaf bract.
Oblanceolate: opposite of lanceolate, widest at the tip and narrow at the base.
Obovate: broad middle and tapered at the base.
Oblong: longer than wide, almost rectangular in shape.
Opposite: the arrangement of leaves on the stem; leaves are attached directly across from each other.
Ovate: egg shape.
Palmate: Palm-like.
Panicle: repeatedly branched inflorescence; a branched raceme.
Pinnate: feather-like, leaflets arranged along each side of the leaf axis.
Pistil: female organ of the flower.
Pod: dry dehiscent fruit.
Pome: fleshy, multi seeded fruit as in apples or pears.
Pubescent: covered in short hairs.
Raceme: an indeterminate inflorescence with pedicel led or stalked flowers.
Samara: dry, indehiscent, winged, fruit structure that contains a seed.
Seed: mature, fertilized embryo.
Semi-evergreen: having green leaves through part of the winter or only part of the plants foliage persists through the winter.
Serrate: toothed, usually refers to a leaf margin.
Sessile: without a stalk.
Simple: leaf that is undivided or entire.
Species: a group of organisms within a genus that are similar and can produce similar offspring, but posses minor variations.
Spike: an elongated, indeterminate inflorescence with sessile flowers.
Stamen: male organ of the flower.
Stem: primary axis of the plant that bears leaves and flowers.
Stoloniferous: bearing stems just above or under the ground; allows a plant to colonize.
Sucker: a shoot that arises from the roots of a plant.
Suckering: producing many suckers, which results in a multi-stemmed plant; allows plants to colonize.
Tendril: twining appendage, which enables plants to climb as *Bignonia*.
Terminal: at the apical or distil end (the tip).
Tomentose: dense, matted, soft hairs.
Variegated: striped, margined, mottled, or any other marking with a color other than green when green is the normal leaf color.
Variety: a subdivision of a species that has a distinct difference.
Vein: the vascular tissue in a leaf.
Venation: the arrangement of the veins in a leaf.
Villous: long soft shaggy hairs (trichomes).

Bibliography

Brickell, Christopher and Judith D. Zuk (ed.). 1996. *The American Horticultural Society A-Z Encyclopedia of Garden Plants*. DK Publishing, Inc. New York, NY.

Dirr, Michael A. 1998. *Manual of Woody Landscape Plants*. Stipes Publishing L.L.C. Champaign, IL.

Foote, Leonard E. and Jones, Samuel B. Jr. 1989. *Native Shrubs and Woody Vines of the Southeast*. Timber Press. Portland, OR.

Godfrey, Robert K. and Jean W. Wooten. 1981. *Aquatic and Wetland Plants of the Southeastern United States: Dicotyledons*. University of Georgia Press. Athens, GA.

Grimm, William Carey. 1966. *Recognizing Native Shrubs*. Stackpole Books. Harrisburg, PA

Head, Bob H. 2006. *Hutchinson's Tree Book: A Reference Guide to Popular Landscape Trees*. Hutchinson Publishing Corporation. Taylors, SC.

Johnson, Warren T. and Lyon, Howard H. 1976. *Insects That Feed on Trees and Shrubs*. Comstock Publishing Associates, a Division of Cornell University Press. Ithaca, New York and London.

Little, Elbert L. 1997. *National Audubon Society Field Guide to Trees: Eastern Region*. Alfred A. Knopf, Inc. New York.

Martin, A. C. Zim, H. S. Nelson, A. L. 1951. *American Wildlife and Plants*. McGraw-Hill Inc. New York

Miller, James H. and Karl V. Miller. 2005. *Forest Plants of the Southeast and Their Wildlife Uses*. University of Georgia Press. Athens, GA.

Niering, William A. and Nancy C. Olmstead. 1995. *National Audubon Society Field Guide to Wildflowers: Eastern Region*. Alfred A. Knopf, Inc. New York.

Pirone, Pascal P. 1978. *Diseases and Pests of Ornamental Plants*. 5th Edition. John Wiley & Sons, Inc. New York, NY.

Radford, Albert E., Harry E. Ahles, and C. Ritchie Bell. 1968. *Manual of the Vascular Flora of the Carolinas*. The University of North Carolina Press. Chapel Hill, NC.

Index to Botanical Names

Acer rubrum **2**, 89, 94, 96
Acer saccharum **3**, 94, 96
Aesculus pavia **37**, 91
Aesculus sylvatica **38**, 91
Alnus serrulata **4**, 89, 96
Amelanchier arborea **5**, 91, 94, 96
Anisostichus capreolatus 83
Aronia arbutifolia **39**, 90, 93, 94, 96
Aronia melanocarpa 39
Asimina triloba **40**, 96
Betula nigra **6**, 89
Bignonia capreolata **83**, 92, 95, 96
Callicarpa americana **41**, 93, 96
Calycanthus floridus **42**, 91
Campis radicans **84**, 92
Carpinus caroliniana **7**, 89, 96
Ceanothus americanus 43, 90, 91, 96
Cephalanthus occidentalis **44**, 89, 91, 96
Cercis canadensis **8**, 91
Chionanthus virginicus **9**, 91, 96
Clethra alnifolia **45**, 89, 91
Cornus amomum **46**, 89, 91, 93, 94, 96
Cornus florida **10**, 91, 93, 94
Decumeria barbara **85**, 89
Diospyros virginiana **11**, 96
Euyonomus americanus **47**, 93
Fagus grandifolia **12**, 96
Fothergilla gardenii 48
Fothergilla major **48**, 91, 94
Fraxinus pennsylvatica **13**, 89
Gelsemium rankinii **86**, 92, 95
Gelsemium sempervirens **87**, 92, 95
Halesia carolina **14**, 89, 91, 93
Hamamelis virginiana **15**, 91, 96
Hydrangea arborescens **49**, 91, 96
Hydrangea quercifolia **50**, 91, 96
Hypericum frondosum **51**, 91
Hypericum densiflorum **52**, 91
Ilex glabra **53**, 95, 96
Ilex opaca **16**, 90, 93, 95, 96
Ilex verticillata **54**, 93, 96
Ilex vomitoria **55**, 90, 93, 95, 96
Illicium floridanum **56**, 89, 91, 95
Illicium parviflorum **57**, 95
Itea virginica **58**, 89, 91, 94
Juniperous virginiana **17**, 90, 95, 96
Kalmia latifolia **59**, 90, 91, 95
Leucothoe axillaris **60**, 89, 91, 95

Leucothoe fontanesiana **61**, 89, 91, 95
Lindera benzoin **62**, 94
Liquidambar styraciflua **18**, 89, 90, 94
Liriodendron tulipifera **19**, 91, 94
Lonicera sempervirens **88**, 92
Magnolia grandiflora **20**, 90, 91, 93, 95
Myrica cerifera **63**, 90, 95, 96
Nyssa sylvatica **21**, 89, 94, 96
Ostrya virginiana **22**, 96
Oxydendron arboreum **23**, 94
Physocarpus opulifolius **64**, 89, 91
Pinus strobus **24**, 95, 96
Platanus occidentalis **25**, 89
Quercus alba **26**, 90, 96
Quercus coccinea **27**, 90, 94, 96
Quercus lyrata **28**, 89, 96
Quercus palustris **29**, 96
Quercus phellos **30**, 90, 96
Quercus prinus **31**, 90, 96
Quercus shumardii **32**, 90, 96
Quercus virginiana **33**, 95, 96
Rhododendron austrinum **65**, 91
Rhododendron calendulaceum **66**, 91
Rhododendron canescens **67**, 91
Rhododendron carolinianum 68, 70
Rhododendron catawbiense **68**, 91, 95
Rhododendron flammeum **69**, 91
Rhododendron minus **70**, 91, 95
Rhododendron viscosum **71**, 89, 91
Sabal palmetto **34**, 89, 93, 95, 96
Sambucus canadensis **72**, 89, 91, 93, 96
Styrax grandifolius **73**, 91
Taxodium distichum **35**, 89
Vaccinium arboreum **74**, 90, 94, 96
Vaccinium ashei **75**, 93, 96
Vaccinium corymbosum **76**, 93, 96
Viburnum acerifolium **77**, 91
Viburnum cassinoides **78**, 91, 93, 94, 96
Viburnum dentatum **79**, 91, 93, 94, 96
Xanthorhiza simplicissima **80**, 89
Yucca filimentosa **81**, 90, 91, 95

Index to Common Names

Adam's Needle **81**, 90, 91, 95
Alder
    Hazel **4**, 89, 96
    Tag **4**
Anise-tree
    Florida **56**, 89, 91, 95
    Yellow **57**, 95
Ash
    Green **13**, 89
Azalea
    Flame **66**, 91
    Florida **65**, 91
    Oconee **69**, 91
    Piedmont **67**, 91
    Swamp **71**, 89, 91
Bald Cypress **35**, 89
Bear-Grass **81**
Beautyberry
    American **41**, 93, 96
Beech
    American **12**, 96
Birch...
    River **6**, 89
Blackgum **21**, 89, 94, 96
Blueberry
    Highbush **76**, 93, 96
    Rabbiteye **75**, 93, 96
    Southern Highbush **75**
Buckeye
    Painted **38**, 91
    Red **37**, 91
Button Bush **44**, 89, 91, 96
Carolina Silverbell **14**, 89, 91, 93
Chokeberry **39**, 90, 93, 94, 96
Climbing Hydrangea **85**, 89
Crossvine **83**, 92, 95, 96
Doghobble
    Coastal **60**, 89, 91, 95
    Piedmont **61**, 89, 91, 95
Dogwood
    Flowering **10**, 91, 93, 94
    Silky **46**, 89, 91, 93, 94, 96
Downy Serviceberry **5**, 91, 94, 96
Eastern Redbud **8**, 91
Eastern Red Cedar **17**, 90, 95, 96
Elderberry **72**, 89, 91, 93, 96

Farkleberry **74**
Fothergilla **48**, 91, 94
Grancy Gray-beard **9**, 91, 96
Hearts a Bursting **47**, 93
Holly
   American **16**, 90, 93, 95, 96
   Inkberry **53**, 95, 96
   Winterberry **54**, 93, 96
   Yaupon **55**, 90, 93, 95, 96
Honeysuckle
   Coral **88**, 92
Hophornbeam
   American **22**, 96
Hornbeam
   American **7**, 89, 96
Hydrangea
   Oakleaf **50**, 91, 96
   Smooth **49**, 91, 96
Jessamine
   Carolina **87**
   Swamp **86**, 92, 95
   Yellow **87**, 92, 95
Magnolia
   Southern **20**, 90, 91, 93, 95
Maple
   Red **2**, 89, 94, 96
   Sugar **3**, 94, 96
Mountain Laurel **59**, 90, 91, 95
New Jersey Tea **43**, 90, 91, 96
Ninebark **64**, 89, 91
Oak
   Chestnut **31**, 90, 96
   Live **33**, 95, 96
   Overcup **28**, 89, 96
   Pin **29**, 96
   Scarlet **27**, 90, 94, 96
   Shumard **32**, 90, 96
   White **26**, 90, 96
   Willow **30**, 90, 96
Palm
   Sabal **34**
Palmetto
   Cabbage **34**, 89, 93, 95, 96
Paw Paw **40**, 96
Persimmon
   Common **11**, 96
Pine
   White **24**, 95, 96
Rhododendron
   Catawba **68**, 91, 95
   Piedmont **70**, 91, 95

Saint Johnswort
- Bushy **52**, 91
- Golden **51**, 91

Serviceberry
- Downy **5**, 91, 94, 96

Snowbell
- Big Leaf **73**, 91

Sourwood **23**, 94

Sparkleberry **74**, 90, 94, 96

Spicebush **62**, 94

Strawberry Bush **47**

Summersweet Clethra **45**, 89, 91

Sweetgum **18**, 89, 90, 94

Sweet Pepper Bush **45**

Sweet Shrub **42**, 91

Sycamore **25**, 89

Trumpet Vine **84**, 92

Tulip Polar **19**, 91, 94

Viburnum
- Arrowwood **79**, 91, 93, 94, 96
- Maple Leaf **77**, 91
- Witherod **78**, 91, 93, 94, 96

Virginia Willow **58**, 89, 91, 94

Wax Myrtle **63**, 90, 95, 96

Witch Hazel
- Common **15**, 91, 96

Yellowroot **80**, 89

ABOUT THE AUTHOR

Michael L. Dorn received a Bachelor of Science in Horticulture and a Master of Science in Botany from Clemson University. During his time as a graduate student and a research associate at Clemson, Michael was involved in a shoreline restoration and wetland research project. Michael propagated and grew native plants for the research project, and he took part in the experimental projects that involved the use of these native plants for erosion control, restoration, and habitat enhancement.

Following his time at Clemson, Michael started Dorn's Landscape Services, LLC, which is a landscape maintenance and design service. In addition to traditional landscape services, Michael also provides a shoreline stabilization design service, which makes it possible for lake property owners to acquire permits to perform shoreline stabilization techniques on their shorelines. All of these designs incorporate native plantings into the stabilization techniques.

In his spare time Michael spends countless hours exploring the rivers, lakes, and forests in the southeastern U.S. to continue his education and understanding of the native ecology and plant life of this beautiful part of the country.

www.ingramcontent.com/pod-product-compliance
Lightning Source LLC
Chambersburg PA
CBHW041550220426
43666CB00002B/29